YANKEE IN GRAY

Henry Ebenezer Handerson in July, 1861,
shortly after his induction into the Confederate Army.
From a daguerrotype in the possession of Mrs. Clarence H. Handerson.

Yankee in Gray

★

THE CIVIL WAR MEMOIRS

OF

Henry E. Handerson

WITH A SELECTION OF HIS WARTIME LETTERS

A BIOGRAPHICAL INTRODUCTION

BY

Clyde Lottridge Cummer

★

The Press of Western Reserve University

———————★———————

Foreword

The Handerson Papers are published as a memorial to Clyde Lottridge Cummer by the Trustees of the Cleveland Medical Library. In doing this, the Trustees honor themselves and the Library just as much as they do Cummer. Cummer was a paragon of wisdom, a genius of administration, a guardian of property, and a pillar of strength almost from the birth of the Library until his death after a period of service of fifty years. Cummer loved the Library and he served it well. For these reasons the Trustees are proud to sponsor publication of this book in the name of Clyde Lottridge Cummer.

The Handerson Memoir was Cummer's final literary project. As a boy, Cummer saw Handerson as a vestryman passing the plate in old Grace Church. As a physician, he recognized the debt of physicians to Handerson for his translation of Johann Hermann Baas, *Grundriss der Geschichte der Medicin und des Heilenden Standes,* Stuttgart, 1876. This was published in English as *Outlines of the History of Medicine and the Medical Profession,* translated and (in conjunction with the author) revised and enlarged, New York, 1889. As a mature citizen, Cummer was intrigued by the personal dilemma of Handerson, a Northern lad without previous Confederate affiliation who was impelled by circumstance to enlist with the Boys in Gray. Cummer appreciated Handerson's hesitancy in coming North to settle after the war, to study medicine, and to practice his profession in what he feared might be a hostile atmosphere.

v

Cummer learned of the Civil War memoirs, sought out surviving Handerson relatives, and obtained the manuscript. He studied the family history, visited the homes, the farms, the places of business which had belonged to Handerson and his relatives. He finally arranged for and attended the graveside memorial services held on May 30, 1956, at Woodland Avenue Cemetery, Cleveland, by the Rt. Rev. Bishop Beverly D. Tucker, Mrs. Walter C. White, representatives of the Handerson family, and the United Daughters of the Confederacy. Small wonder it is that Cummer strove so enthusiastically to work out the story completely, told it so many times to different audiences and was determined to publish it. This he was prevented from doing only by his untimely death.

Cummer had not prepared the material for final publication. Genevieve Miller has been completely responsible for this, and to her goes the credit for the final revision which she has done so well. She edited and annotated the manuscript, checked the references, selected the illustrations, and dealt with the publisher. The text has been reproduced as Handerson wrote it, the only editorial changes being some revisions in spelling and capitalization. Our thanks go to the Western Reserve University Press and particularly to Willis Thornton, the Director, for the resulting memorial volume.

ROBERT M. STECHER, M.D.

February 14, 1962

Contents

Henry E. Handerson

Henry E. Handerson in later years,
a scholar devoted
to the history of medicine.

Henry E. Handerson

A CAREER OF CONTRASTS

Henry E. Handerson's long life spanned a swiftly moving period in the history of the United States. Beginning in the panic year of 1837 and stretching eighty-one years almost to the end of World War I, he saw his nation engaged in four wars and actively participated in one of them himself. His life, like his character, was full of striking contrasts. Born and bred in northeastern Ohio—the district known as the Western Reserve of Connecticut whose early settlers were imbued with New England ways of thinking—he fought, bled, and was imprisoned for the Confederate cause. This period of military hazards formed an interlude between early study and teaching and the later placid life of student, physician, historian, and classical scholar. During his professional career he witnessed and helped record revolutionary discoveries in medicine—the "germ theory" of disease, Roentgen rays, and aseptic surgery. His scholarly proclivities were not incompatible with administrative zeal and shrewd practical sense in money matters. In spite of the agnostic tendencies of his time he remained an active and devout churchman.

Those who remember him recall a distinguished, tall, slender gentleman with a white beard. He often wore a black skull cap, as did many men with thinning pates in those days. He was usually dressed in a long black coat of the Prince Albert type, a white vest, and a white bow necktie. That is the way I recall him as he collected the offertory at the old Grace Episcopal Church. Always dignified, he was urbane and courteous, at times genial. He was truly, as Dr. W. E. Bruner described him, a "gentleman of the old

3

school."[1] His venerable and stately appearance was appropriate for his position as church-warden. Seeing him in church or presiding over the sedate meetings of the Cleveland Medical Library Association, no one would have pictured him as "a fiery, youthful Confederate officer, leading a charge at a run up-hill over fallen logs and brush, sounding the 'Rebel yell,' leaping a hedge and alighting in a ten-foot ditch among Federal troopers who surrounded him and his comrades."[2]

The Handersons were New Englanders whose first appearance in Colonial records was in Hartford, Connecticut, about 1694. Dr. Handerson's great-great-grandfather Gideon Handerson eventually settled in Amherst, Massachusetts, where in 1762 he purchased a farm of ninety-five acres which remained the home of the Handerson family for almost a century. It now forms part of the grounds of the University of Massachusetts, while the President's residence occupies the site of Gideon Handerson's home.

Gideon was a selectman and a member of the Revolutionary Committee of Amherst. His son Timothy (Dr. Handerson's great-grandfather) served as a corporal in the Revolutionary War. Timothy's son Ira lived for a time in Claverack, Columbia County, New York but in 1834 was caught up in the great Western movement and brought his wife and family to the rolling country of Orange Township, Cuyahoga County, Ohio. His son Thomas, the father of Dr. Handerson, was then thirty years old, married, and the father of three children.[3]

The family became well known in the Chagrin Valley. A great uncle, Dr. Seth Smith Handerson, together with Noah Graves had laid out the village of Chagrin Falls in 1833 and was later sheriff of the county. One of Dr. Handerson's sisters, Caroline Marian, married Washington Gates, the first white child born in the village of Gates Mills. His aunt Eliza married Frederick Willson, a well-known farmer and miller of Willson's Mills in adjoining Mayfield Township.

The Handerson homestead, occupied by the family for four generations, still stands at the corner of Fairmount and River Roads, about fifteen miles east of Cleveland's Public Square and three miles south of Gates Mills, a quaint village like a bit of transplanted New England with its spired white church, broad village green, and neat white frame houses surrounded by white picket fences.[4] River Road follows the west bank of the river, running north and south through the farm which extended from the river's edge up the hillside.

[1]Superior figures refer to Notes to the Text which begin on page 121.

The river played a tragic part in the history of the family. It is reported that when Thomas' wife (née Catherine Potts) first saw the Chagrin River flowing in front of her new home in 1834 "an irrepressible shudder seized her, and a premonition of evil crept over her." Less than a year later, on July 4, 1835, her five-year-old son William was accidentally drowned in the river. In June 1839 her husband died from a fractured spine incurred while bathing in the river, and when he died his widow "felt that her aversion had been prophetic."[5]

Henry Ebenezer Handerson was born in the family homestead on March 21, 1837.[6] After his father's death he and his sister Harriet were adopted by his father's brother, Lewis Handerson, and his wife (née Prudence Punderson) who had no children of their own. The young adopted children moved to their home in Cleveland in the fall of 1839. Lewis Handerson was prominent in the city's business life and highly respected. He had learned the drug business in Hudson, N.Y., and, having formed a partnership with his future brother-in-law, Ebenezer Punderson, Jr., had come to Cleveland and opened a drug store with the arresting name of Handerson and Punderson.[7] One of the incorporators of the Society for Savings in 1849, he served on its first board of trustees from 1849 to 1852. He was a warden of early Trinity Church. The newspapers show him as an active Whig.

Prudence Punderson Handerson, with her brothers Ebenezer and the Rev. Ephraim Punderson, must have had much influence on the formation of Henry E. Handerson's character. His uncle Ebenezer lived with the Handersons, and the Rev. Ephraim probably visited them often on his journeys in Northern Ohio as an Episcopal missionary.[8]

Geographically the Handerson interests were well concentrated. The drug store was on Superior Street between Seneca and Bank Streets (now West Third and West Sixth Streets). Around the corner on Seneca was the home, and still further north at the southeast corner of St. Clair (the site now occupied by the Hawley House) was their church, Trinity Episcopal, the first church building to be erected in Cleveland. Later the family moved to 173 St. Clair Street (old numbering) and the Society for Savings Bank opened its first office at 4 Bank Street around the corner from the drug store. Henry Handerson has described the Cleveland of his boyhood as follows:[9]

"The city of Cleveland contained a population of about 10,000 souls. Nine years before it had with due ceremony donned the municipal toga, and now, with infinite scorn, it looked down upon the poor 2,500 inhabitants of its ancient and formidable rival across the Cuyahoga, then known under the

Captain Henry E. Handerson
in June, 1865, immediately after his release
from a Federal prison camp.

ambitious title of Ohio City. The city proper was bounded on the East by Erie (now East Ninth) and on the south by Bolivar, and though our present Euclid Avenue had begun to display evidence of its future grandeur, the great majority of our solid citizens occupied homes in what is now called the 'down-town district' [between St. Clair Street and the lake and between the river and Ontario Street]. No ambitious city airs disturbed the peace of the quiet inhabitants. Cows roamed at will through the unpaved streets or browsed the tender grass of the numerous vacant lots, and the cosmopolitan pig luxuriated undisturbed in the mud of the undrained gutters. Honest citizens retired to their couches at nine o'clock, guided to their homes by domestic instinct rather than by any artificial light, while no screaming of locomotive whistles nor rumble of horse-cars vexed the repose of the matutinal slumberer. The river bottom then bore the ignominious title of 'The Flats,' and was the chosen home of the melodious frog and the pasture-land of the city kine, who were driven every night and morning to and from their homes by bare-footed and bare-headed youths, the substantial business men of this year of grace."

Henry Handerson was a frail boy and could attend school only part of the time. At the age of fourteen he entered Sanger Hall, a boarding-school at New Hartford, Oneida County, New York, conducted by his foster-uncle, the Rev. Ephraim Punderson, but he was obliged to withdraw because of his health. In 1851 the firm of Handerson and Punderson, having carried on its business "with a highly honorable reputation" for twenty years, sold out to S. E. Strong and A. C. Armstrong.[10] The following year the Lewis Handersons moved from Cleveland to Beersheba Springs, Grundy County, Tennessee, where Lewis Handerson built a delightful home on the summit of one of the ranges of the Cumberland Mountains, not far from Chattanooga and Signal Mountain.

In 1854 Henry, restored in health, returned to Cleveland and prepared for Hobart College, Geneva, N.Y., from which he graduated in 1858. It is significant that at the commencement exercises he delivered the "philosophical oration" on the subject of "The Historian."[11] Returning to Tennessee he busied himself for about a year with surveying and similar pursuits in the vicinity of his home, and in 1859 he accepted a position as private tutor to the family of Washington Compton, a cotton planter of Alexandria, Louisiana.

The details of his life between 1859 and the summer of 1865 are vividly recorded in a memoir which he wrote for his family in the 1890's and which

7

is published here for the first time together with letters which he wrote to Lewis Handerson describing his wartime experiences.

After the war Handerson entered the College of Physicians and Surgeons in New York and received the degree of doctor of medicine in 1867.[12] In 1866 his alma mater, Hobart, had conferred on him the M.A. degree. He practiced on Lexington Avenue in New York until 1885. From 1869 to 1872 he was Assistant Surgeon of the Hospital for the Ruptured and Crippled. In 1872 he married Juliet Alice Root. Tragedy was again his lot. His wife died in 1881 after giving birth to her fourth child. In the following year his three older children, aged eight, six, and five years, died within five days of each other from what was then called "black diphtheria." Dr. Handerson returned to Cleveland with his remaining daughter, Juliet Alice, in 1885, and on June 12, 1888, he married Clara Corlett of Cleveland. By this marriage he had two sons, Clarence H. and Philip C.[13]

While in New York Handerson had become interested in medical history. In 1878 he read a paper to the Medical Society of the County of New York on "The School of Salernum, an Historical Sketch of Mediaeval Medicine" which was published as a sixty-page pamphlet in 1883. A scholarly contribution based on extensive research, it attracted wide attention and served to introduce Handerson as a medical historian. Fielding H. Garrison described it as a "solid piece of original investigation, worthy to be placed beside such things as Holmes on homoeopathy, Weir Mitchell on instrumental precision, or Kelly on American gynecology."[14]

Handerson's *magnum opus* appeared in 1889 in the form of the American edition of *Outlines of the History of Medicine and the Medical Profession* by Joh. Hermann Baas, M.D., translated, and in conjunction with the author revised and enlarged, by H. E. Handerson, M.A., M.D. The copyright was taken out in Dr. Handerson's name. In the preface the self-designated translator, in reality the co-author, states that "No pains have been spared to render the names, dates, etc., as accurate as possible, but in a work involving such an infinity of details of this nature it would be unreasonable to expect that some errors and omissions should not be found. For these the translator can merely beg the mantle of that charity which, according to the apostle, 'shall cover the multitude of sins.'" Of this work Fielding H. Garrison said: "To the cognoscenti, Dr. Handerson's translation of Baas' *History of Medicine* (1889) is known as 'Handerson's Book.' He modestly describes himself as its 'editor,' but he is more than that. As the witty and effective translator of a witty and effective work, he has added sections in brackets on English

8

and American history which are based on original investigation and are of permanent value to all future historians. Handerson's Baas is thus more complete and valuable than the Rhinelander's original text."[15]

The list of Handerson's other writings is not long. His work was too painstakingly laborious to be voluminous. Included are papers dealing with sanitation, vital statistics, and the diseases of Cleveland. Contributions of great value about local history appeared in Orth's *History of Cleveland,* and similar if not identical material in the *Cleveland Medical Journal.*[16] Here one finds a narrative of medicine in early Cleveland with references to pioneer physicians and sections on medical societies, medical colleges, public hygiene, epidemics, and the early pest-house. It is obvious that he had carried out tedious research in the minute books of the early societies and in old newspaper files. Had it not been for Handerson, probably almost all traces of the local medical past would have been lost forever.

Handerson made other valuable contributions to Ohio's medical history, which appeared in twenty-seven biographical sketches in Howard A. Kelly's *Cyclopedia of American Medical Biography* (1912). The accounts of Jared P. Kirtland, Noah Worcester, Horace A. Ackley, John Lang Cassels, John Delamater, Theodatus Garlick, John S. Newberry, and Samuel St. John are of particular interest. Few Cleveland physicians were included by Handerson in his translation of Baas' history, an example of his sense of perspective, for although the city had its fair share of excellent teachers and practitioners, those whose contributions had up to that time influenced the course of medical history were scarce.

Although ostensibly in retirement, Handerson served as Professor of Hygiene and Sanitary Science in the Medical Department of the University of Wooster from 1894 to 1896 and held the same chair in its successor institution, the Cleveland College of Physicians and Surgeons, the medical department of Ohio Wesleyan, from 1896 to 1907.[17]

His special interest in the field of public health may have resulted from the toll which diphtheria had levied on his family, and from his experiences with disease in army life. Dr. S. W. Kelley, a contemporary faculty member, said that he filled the chair with eminent ability.[18] We may be sure that his teaching had a broadly philosophical and historical background which few could have supplied. Among his papers are eight lectures devoted to a survey of medical history through the eighteenth century.

No account of Handerson's life could be adequate without reference to his religion. Handerson's inclinations which had been fostered by the Pundersons doubtless were strengthened during his days at Hobart College (Episcopal) to which he was devotedly loyal to the end of his days. When he returned to live in Cleveland in 1885 he went back to the family church, Grace Episcopal,[19] and in 1890 we find him as a delegate from his parish to the diocesan convention, in 1890 to 1891 as clerk of the vestry and in 1893 as junior warden. Four years later he was made senior warden, a post he held until 1917. During the period from 1892 to 1913 he represented his parish eighteen times in the diocesan conventions.[20] In addition Handerson held the responsible position of diocesan treasurer from 1903 to 1916 and served on the diocesan finance committee. He was a staunch supporter of the free pew system, stoutly opposing the rental of pews and advocating free will offerings. In his usual scholarly style he wrote a history of the parish in a booklet published in 1898.[21]

His devotion to his faith is noteworthy since his was the era when Darwinism rocked the Christian world. Many men of scientific education and inclinations were re-examining their religious beliefs not only in the light of evolutionary hypotheses but also of current critical Biblical research, with the result that many became agnostic. In Baas' book Darwinism is discussed, but apparently by Baas himself, so that we have no indication of how Handerson met this challenge to orthodoxy.

He was not a Sunday-only Christian. There were family devotions each morning which lasted at least thirty minutes when the first and second lessons were read as prescribed by the Book of Common Prayer. Long graces were said before each meal. Young guests of his children were expected to attend morning devotions no matter how late they had been up at college dances the night before, and they were summoned in no uncertain way.

During his Cleveland years Handerson did not carry on a medical practice and saw only a few old friends or acquaintances professionally in his home. His energies were devoted to studies, writing, teaching, medical society activities, and his church. He was typically the student and recluse. A family member has said that when he was working in the library of his home it was understood that no one was to enter without knocking.

His active interest in medical society work was shown by his regular attendance at the meetings of the old Cuyahoga County Medical Society. He presented papers rather frequently, served as President in 1895-1896, and was one of the first group of trustees of its successor, the Academy of Medicine, when it was organized in 1902.[22]

His services in the formation and development of the Cleveland Medical

Library Association were outstanding. This institution was established in 1894 by the action of a joint committee appointed from the three medical societies then in existence in Cleveland. The old and conservative Cuyahoga County Medical Society was represented by Drs. Henry E. Handerson, Marcus Rosenwasser, and Henry W. Rogers; the small and exclusive Cleveland Academy of Medical Sciences by Drs. Isaac Himes, Benjamin L. Millikin, and Dudley P. Allen; the new and bustling Cleveland Medical Society by Drs. W. H. Humiston, J. E. Cook, and P. Maxwell Foshay. The first treasurer resigned after being in office but a few months and Handerson was elected in his place. The following year he was made President and he continued in office for seven years until 1902. He served on almost every committee in the early days; the list of appointments bespeaks his great interest.[23]

That Cleveland has its medical library of today is in large part due to the efforts of Handerson, and it was most fitting that when the new library building was erected in 1926, the building committee designated the very heart of the library, its book stacks, as the Henry E. Handerson Book Stacks, hanging his portrait near the entrance to the stacks in the Cushing Reading Room. When this building was opened formally Dr. Harvey Cushing, one of Cleveland's distinguished sons, said in the dedication address: "It was in this way that the nucleus of your historical collection came to be deposited here as the gift of that remarkable and cultured man, Dr. H. E. Handerson, your one medical historian of note—a man whose memory you will increasingly come to honor."[24] Handerson therefore deserves a place of great honor in Cleveland medical history as a founder of the two major medical organizations which continue to this day, The Academy of Medicine of Cleveland (the county medical society) and the Cleveland Medical Library Association.[25]

The last research in which Handerson engaged was a careful analytical study of the *Compendium Medicinae* of Gilbertus Anglicus, a famous medieval English physician, one of the "authorities" of Chaucer's Doctor of Phisik: "Bernard and Gatesdan and Gilbertyn." A short paper on Gilbert was published in *Medical Pickwick*,[26] while an extensive paper had been set in type for the *Cleveland Medical Journal*. Increasing difficulty with his eyesight prevented Handerson from reading proof, and publication was deferred at his insistence. However, it was published posthumously by the Cleveland Medical Library Association as a monograph with a biographical foreword by Samuel W. Kelley.[27]

In June 1915, fifty years after Lee's surrender, Handerson attended a meeting in Richmond, Va., of his old Confederate comrades who had suffered imprisonment together. They relived the days of gallant fighting and the ordeals of imprisonment. A little band of twenty-four out of the original six hundred attended. Some of the veterans met with the group for the first time since their release from Fort Delaware as paroled prisoners of war. When the Roll Call of the Dead had been read, Comrade H. E. Handerson arose in his place and answered for the dead comrades, "Absent, but accounted for, safe with the Immortals."[28]

This was his last journey away from home. In 1916 he became blind. The total darkness of his last two years was born with "unvarying patience and cheerfulness."[29] He still loved to recite from memory the classical authors, to relate and discuss episodes in world history and events of the present, to solve difficult mathematical problems, and to have his data on all subjects verified. His family read the newspapers to him, so that he could follow the progress of World War I—he was interested especially in military strategy. His mental faculties were retained perfectly until April 23, 1918, when he died from cerebral hemorrhage.[30]

ACKNOWLEDGMENT

I received assistance from William Ganson Rose, author of *Cleveland, the Making of a City,* in producing the manuscript of Handerson's Civil War Memoir, his letters to his foster father and other memorabilia from Dr. Handerson's surviving son, Mr. Philip C. Handerson of Delray, Florida. Mrs. Ernestine Handerson, widow of the elder son Clarence, aided materially with reminiscences of Dr. Handerson's family life and also in procuring the loan of photographs, manuscripts and some of the books quoted. The Venerable Archdeacon Wonders made available to me certain official records of the Cathedral headquarters in Cleveland. Mrs. Walter C. White secured transcripts of official records. Dr. Genevieve Miller gave advice regarding the preparation of the manuscript.

CLYDE L. CUMMER, M.D.

Yankee in Gray

★

Forsan et haec olim meminisse juvabit. VERGIL[1]

The following pages have been written for the information and amusement of my children, and particularly to preserve to them some reminiscences of the struggle now known as the "Great Rebellion"— the desperate and bloody contest between the North and South which convulsed this land for four years, 1861-1865, and which has left its impress upon the politics and social life of the country down even to the present day.[2] Indeed, it is doubtful whether even a century will fully obliterate the prejudices and misconceptions then generated, or rather then fully developed and fructified. A brief sketch of my life prior to the late war will form a useful introduction.

[1]Superior figures refer to Notes to the Text which begin on page 124.

THE CIVIL WAR MEMOIRS OF

Henry E. Handerson

EARLY LIFE

I was born on Tuesday, March 21, 1837, in the town of Orange, Cuyahoga Co., Ohio, near the point now known as "Henderson's Cross-Roads" on the Chagrin river. My father, Thomas Handerson, immigrated to Ohio from Columbia Co., New York, in 1834, and settled upon a farm adjoining that of his father, Ira Handerson, in the town of Orange. His letters show him to have been a man of moderate education and sterling sense, and he is reported to have been highly esteemed and respected by his neighbors. While bathing in the Chagrin River, near the village now known as "Gates's Mills" or "the Point," he accidentally struck his head against a sunken snag with such force as to fracture his spine and produce paralysis of his entire body below the neck, a condition which resulted in his death after a few days, on June 4th, 1839. My mother, thus left a widow with five children, the eldest at this time only thirteen years of age, was of course stunned by the sudden and unexpected blow. She was, however, a woman of great decision of character and good sense, and, after the first effects of the shock had passed away, bravely faced the difficult task of providing for her youthful family. My father's brother, Lewis Handerson, was at this time a druggist in Cleveland, and as he and his wife had no children, he proposed to my mother to adopt her two younger children, Harriet Frances and myself, thus providing for them, and at the same time lightening somewhat the burden of my mother. After some hesitation she consented to the arrangement, and in the Fall of 1839 we were brought to our new home in Cleveland. Here we were brought up with every care, and treated with as much affection as we could have been by our natural parents.

EDUCATION

In spite of a sickly childhood, I managed to attend school with considerable regularity, and, at the age of about fourteen was sent to a boarding-school[3] at New Hartford, near Utica, N. Y., where my adopted mother's brother, the Rev. Ephraim Punderson, was engaged in teaching. Here my health became so poor that I was compelled to withdraw from school, and, as my adopted father had meanwhile sold out his business in Cleveland and made arrangements to remove to Tennessee, I returned in the Spring of 1852 to Cleveland, and, in company with Mr. Ebenezer Punderson (another brother of my adopted mother), my mother and sister Harriet, we drove in our private conveyance from the city of Cleveland to Beersheba Springs,[4] Grundy Co., Tennessee, where my adopted father had decided to make his new home. Here I remained for about two years, when, as my health seemed quite restored, I returned in the Spring of 1854 to Cleveland and began my preparations for entering college. In September 1854 I matriculated in Hobart Free College, Geneva, N. Y., and completed my course in that institution, graduating in 1858. Returning at once to Tennessee, I occupied myself for about a year in surveying land and similar pursuits in the vicinity of my home, when the offer of a position as private tutor in the family of Mr. Washington Compton, of Alexandria, Louisiana, induced me to settle in that state.

A PRIVATE TUTOR

Accordingly, in the summer of 1859 I set out for my new home, travelling as far as Memphis by rail. At this period railroads were by no means so numerous as at the present day, and it was necessary for me to take a steamer down the Mississippi to the mouth of Red River, and thence, a steamer of lighter draught up the Red River to Alexandria. The regular packet steamers on the Mississippi were models of elegance and comfort in those days, and though large, were built with flat bottoms so as to float readily over the numerous bars of the river in times of low water. It was a novel and amusing sight to me to observe the huge steamer sail slowly up to the river bank and drop a passenger almost at his own door and on his own plantation, very much as one of our omnibuses deposits a passenger upon his own sidewalk in the city.

The Mississippi steamers of that period were also notorious as places of rendezvous for gamblers, pickpockets and similar gentry, and on boarding the floating palace which was to convey me to the mouth of Red River, I quietly determined to have little or nothing to do with my fellow-passengers, in order to avoid falling into bad company. Accordingly I spent most of my time by day upon the bow of the steamer, reading or watching the scenery, or observing the novel spectacle of taking on cotton-bales at the various landings. A very quiet and gentlemanlike man, apparently about thirty or thirty-five years of age, frequently took a seat near me and busied himself with reading or watching the ever-shifting scenes, and gradually there sprung up between us a mild acquaintanceship and intimacy, founded apparently upon a similarity of tastes and habits of thought. My friend was very neatly, but by no means showily, dressed, wore a nicely trimmed beard, had a bright and piercing black eye, and conversed like a man of education and refinement. I rarely saw him except in the morning and at our usual rendezvous on the bow of the boat, where he appeared regularly about 11 A.M., book in hand and smoking a cigar. I could not avoid feeling some curiosity as to who my new acquaintance might be, but, of course, asked him no questions. My conjectures relative to his character fluctuated between a wealthy gentleman of leisure, travelling for pleasure and information, and a professional man, perhaps a U. S. senator or representative, en route for home. The night before leaving the steamer I went into the barber-shop to get shaved, and, looking curiously into an adjoining room, from which arose the noise of numerous voices, I beheld for the first time a faro table, with its piles of colored counters and money, and behind it, with his coat off, shuffling the cards and intent upon the business of the hour—my acquaintance of the morning hours, dealing faro!! My youthful vanity as a student of character received, then and there, a shock from which it never recovered.

JOURNEY UP THE RED RIVER

The next afternoon, about four o'clock, we reached the mouth of Red River, and I landed upon a little wooden dock and wended my way to a small one-story house, the only building in sight, which proved to be a sort of cross between a country store and an inn. My inquiries as to when the steamer up Red River would arrive elicited the rather unsatisfactory information that the water in the river was so low that the steamers were

17

unable to run with anything like regularity, and that the next boat up the river might arrive that night, or not for a day or two. I looked about me with some dismay, wondering where I could possibly make my home in so forlorn-looking a place. The low and level river bank, with its black and boggy soil, was fringed with large trees, whose spreading branches waved in a dismal and sombre dignity long wreaths of grayish moss, as if in funereal pomp. The inn itself was small and uninviting, half of the building being devoted, as I have said, to the purposes of a country store, whose attractions had collected half a dozen or more of the young men of the vicinity, whose horses were tied to various trees, or hitched to a rack in front of the building. Occasionally, however, a stylish equipage drove up under the guidance of a more or less liveried Negro, flanked often on either side by a well-dressed, good-looking young man on horseback, and occupied by one or more ladies, who were availing themselves of the coolness of the evening to enjoy a pleasant drive, procure the mail left by the last steamer and revel in the luxury of a slight flirtation. All the sights and sounds around me were so different from those to which I had been accustomed that a feeling of isolation and sadness crept over me, and the prospect of spending a day or two in this mournful place seemed almost intolerable.

Fortunately, about 10 o'clock at night the lights of the Red River steamer appeared on the river below, and with a lightened heart I hastened on board. The boat was very small, to correspond with the volume of water in the river, and contrast with the magnificent steamer which I had recently left made her seem a veritable pigmy. As I entered the saloon I was shocked to find the whole cabin filled with long dining-tables, at each of which sat a number of men busily engaged in playing cards and drinking. Ah, thought I, now indeed I have fallen into a den of thieves and gamblers. The majority of the players were rather roughly dressed, had long hair and unkempt beards, chewed tobacco with devotion and spat into the spittoons scattered around the floor with an accuracy born of long practice. On the whole, a more unattractive company it had never been my fortune to meet. However, as my eyes adapted themselves to the brilliant light of the cabin, I observed that no money was visible upon the tables, and subsequent experience informed me that the majority of the card-players were respectable country-planters, returning from a visit to their agents in New Orleans. As soon as a berth had been assigned to me I went to my stateroom, and was by no means pleased to find the upper berth already occupied by a stranger, who peered down curiously upon me, at the same time pushing his hand nervously under his pillow, as if to make sure of the security of his valuables and his revolver. The hint was not lost upon me, and, having arranged my treasures and defensive weapon in a similar manner, I crept into my berth and lay awake for a long time, nervous from the novel experiences of the day. At last, however, nature asserted her rights, and I fell into a profound sleep, lasting until after daylight the next morning.

On awaking, the sound of hurrying feet and numerous voices on deck convinced me that something unusual was occurring, and, having hastily donned my clothing, I hurried through the empty cabin to the upper deck, where another novel sight awaited me. The river, at the point where we stopped, appeared not more than a hundred yards in width, and its surface was marked by numerous ripples which indicated the shallowness of the water. While looking upon the scene with interest I was astonished to see two of the deck-hands roll up their pants above the knee, seize the end of a stout rope and plunge into the water, which did not seem to be more than two feet deep. Wading along to the shore, they scrambled up the bank and made fast the end of the rope to a stout tree upon the river-bank. This tree stood considerably ahead of the steamer, and when the rope had been firmly secured around its trunk, I saw that the other end passed over the capstan of the steamer. A moment after the capstan, which was turned by steam, began to revolve, the rope tightened and the steamer began slowly to advance, actually dragged over the gravelly bottom of "the bar" by the revolution of the capstan. This was to me a new method of steam-locomotion. About noon we reached Alexandria and I went to the best-looking hotel for my dinner.

COMPTON'S PLANTATION

Soon after dinner a gray-headed old Negro in a coarse cotton shirt and very seedy pants accosted me and inquired if I was "the teacher." On receiving an affirmative reply, he said the carriage was waiting for me, and, having taken possession of my trunk, he led the way to that vehicle. The latter, a very dilapidated "rock-away," drawn by one horse, was standing at the door, and, perhaps in reply to a somewhat amused look on my part, my ancient guide rather apologized for the appearance of his vehicle by saying that the "carriage" was at present employed by the family, and that he had, therefore, been compelled to come for me with the present conveyance. Our route to the plantation, which lay about five miles from the town of Alexandria, ran along the banks of the Bayou Rapides, a sluggish and muddy stream fringed with bushes and trees; but the road was good, and, as we passed between lofty and untrimmed hedges of the Osage orange or beneath the shelter of the moss-wreathed trees, I thought I had never seen a more lovely country road. On the way we passed a large sugar-plantation, the cane standing about as high as my head and beautifully green, and, as I looked upon it with great interest and made numerous inquiries about its cultivation, the old Negro, who seemed to feel the responsibility for my proper entertainment resting for the moment upon his shoulders, suddenly stopped his horse, and handing me the lines, jumped over the fence, cut a few stalks of the cane and at once initiated me into the process of sucking out the sugary sap, a process which seemed to afford him solid satisfaction and certainly offered me the charm of entire novelty.

We soon arrived at Mr. Compton's plantation and stopped in front of the owner's mansion. This was a two-story and basement house of ample proportions, but with little pretensions to architectural beauty. The basement story was of brick, the remainder of wood, and the entire front, like most southern houses, was provided with a roomy verandah. The house stood about a hundred yards from the road, from which it was separated by a handsome grassy lawn, dotted with a few large trees. I was at once conducted to the parlor and introduced to the family and to some visitors who happened to be present. Mr. Compton, a man apparently about 45 years of age with a semi-military air, erect and alert in his movements, handsome except for a certain air of sternness, not to say cruelty, about his mouth, received me with the genuine cordiality of a Southern gentleman, and did his best to make me feel at home. His wife had evidently been a handsome woman in her youth, and preserved even yet some traces of beauty, though her face bore the marks of the fretfulness of chronic invalidism. She received me politely, but with a sort of cold curiosity that I did not particularly admire. The remainder of the family consisted of a daughter Kate, apparently about 23-24 years of age, not a beauty, but graceful in her carriage and kind of manner: a son John, about 21, hearty and full of life, who soon became a warm friend: another son George, about 17, thoughtful and studious, and five younger children: Ernest, Angus, Blanche (a sweet little girl of about nine years), with two younger boys, Clarence and Walter. The latter six constituted my pupils. George, however, was soon fitted to enter the State Military Academy[5], an institution just organized near Alexandria, and at this

20

period under the direction of the late famous General (then Major) W. T. Sherman.

A small frame house on one side of the lawn served as my schoolroom, and here I spent most of the day engaged in the rather monotonous routine of teaching the primary English branches. About 4 P.M. I dismissed my school, and usually took a ride on horseback for an hour or more along the banks of the bayou, which ran in front of the house. At tea I rejoined the family, and our evenings were commonly spent upon the verandah, the gentlemen smoking and chatting with the ladies until about 9 o'clock. On Saturday John Compton and I frequently went duck-hunting along Red River, or visited some of the young men of the neighborhood, and on Sunday we usually attended church in Alexandria, the ladies going in the carriage, the gentlemen on horseback. Mr. Compton's plantation, which embraced perhaps 200-250 acres, was devoted to the cultivation of cotton, and occupied some 50-60 Negroes, who lived in "quarters," i.e. a dozen or more comfortable log cabins about half a mile in rear of the house.

COMMENTS ON SLAVERY

As an example of a form of civilization which has now largely disappeared from our country, it may be well to say a few words about slavery as it appeared to my observation. Most of the Negroes were fat, lazy fellows, indisposed to do anything more than was absolutely required of them, but rarely giving serious trouble. Often, after their day's labor was completed, the sound of the violin and the shuffle of the merry dancers at the "quarters" bore witness to the lightness of their hearts and the elasticity of their muscles. Men and women labored together in the fields, clad in coarse gray home-spun cloth, and with their heads protected by an old straw or felt hat, or a red bandana handkerchief. Every morning the daily ration of corn-meal and bacon was served out by the master or mistress at the house and conveyed thence in a cart or upon the shoulders to the "quarters," where it was prepared by the old women for the meals of the laborers. The Negroes also kept their own poultry, and often made considerable pocket-money by selling eggs and chickens to the mistress of the house. In sickness they were attended by the family physician and nursed by one of the old women or other person detailed for that purpose. As a rule their treatment was humane, nor were they by any means overworked.

21

The great curse of the system was the management by overseers, usually ignorant and unprincipled whites, to whose carelessness and brutality the indolent masters frequently consigned their slaves. The smaller planters, however, like Mr. Compton, usually managed their own plantations and treated their Negroes well. Even Mr. Compton, however, employed for a time an ignorant Kentuckian as overseer, and I suspect that he was occasionally harsh and tyrannical, though no direct evidence to this effect ever came to my observation. Indeed, I never saw a slave whipped, though on one occasion I heard Mr. Compton himself whipping his house-servant Jeff, an intelligent, but rather morose Negro of perhaps 35 years. Mr. Compton was a man of violent temper when aroused, and looked a very devil on these occasions, but this particular whipping at least was neither long nor severe. Jeff was a good-looking Negro and very popular among the girls of the neighboring plantations, and I suspect that some escapade in this line was the occasion of the castigation which I overheard.

Two Negro children about 8 or 10 years of age were employed in the house as house-servants, besides those occupied in the kitchen. Miss Kate Compton had a little girl called Clarissa for her body-servant, but as Clarissa was usually asleep, I fancy she could have been of little service to her mistress, except in occasionally saving her a few steps. A boy blackened the boots, carried wood and attended to other light jobs, usually sleeping before the fire in my room with his head between his knees and toward the fire, and his breech stuck up in the air. If he had any permanent bed it must have been rarely occupied. He very rarely said anything except "yes, Sir" and "no, Sir," and was altogether a rather weird and goblin-like personage. Once in a while a Methodist preacher made his appearance at the house to preach to the Negroes, who, on such occasions, were all invited to the house, the basement-hall of which was converted into a temporary meeting-house. The family and all guests also attended these meetings, and many ludicrous scenes were witnessed on these occasions, though the earnestness and devoutness of the colored audience made great amends for their ignorance. Once I recollect "old uncle Peter," the aged Negro who drove me over from Alexandria, having been called upon by the minister to lead the Negroes in prayer, began in solemn tones to repeat the Lord's Prayer, in which we all united with becoming reverence until the petition "Forgive us this day our daily bread" tempted our risibilities beyond control. Uncle Peter, be it known, was a notorious thief, and also the conveyor of the daily rations from the house to the Negro-quarters, and it had been hinted, more than

22

once, that Peter frequently increased his own supply of "daily bread" at the expense of the rations of his associates.

MEDICAL STUDENT IN NEW ORLEANS

Amid such scenes I passed a pleasant life until the Fall of 1860, when I resigned my position as private tutor, and, in company with John Compton, went to New Orleans to attend a course of medical lectures. We found a boarding-house on Carondelet Street, and at once matriculated in what was then called the Medical Department of the University of Louisiana, but is now known as Tulane University.[6] This school was then in its prime, and among its professors were the famous and eccentric Warren Stone[7], T. G. Richardson[8], Dr. Cenas[9] and Dr. Hunt[10], and the Faculty, as a whole, was undoubtedly the best in the South. Dr. Davidson[11] of Alexandria, with whom both young Compton and I had studied, had given me a letter of introduction to Dr. Stone, and some ten days after my arrival in New Orleans I proceeded to his private hospital on Canal St. and, with considerable trepidation, presented my letter. The Doctor was very busy with his patients at the time, but glanced over the letter and shaking me cordially by the hand said, heartily but gruffly, "Come in to see me, Handerson, whenever you want to. Don't be afraid of being in the way. If you are I will tell you so," and turned at once to his professional duties. A man of great ability and the kindest of hearts, Dr. Stone was fairly worshipped by the people of New Orleans, who regarded his professional dictum as the law of the Medes and Persians, and laughed at his gruffness and eccentricities as the peculiarities of genius. Dr. Cenas was of French descent and full of the gesture and grimace of that volatile people, while Dr. Hunt was something of a "dandy," frequently appearing in full dress with kid gloves to perform the dirty work of a post mortem before the medical class.

Compton and I had been joined by an intimate friend, Penn Crain, of the parish of Natchitoches, and we three devoted our time quite faithfully to study and attendance upon the regular course of medical lectures. Our few intervals of leisure were, of course, devoted to seeing the sights of New Orleans, and many a pleasant stroll we took through the older portions of this quaint old city, enjoying a cup of delicious coffee in the famous "French market," occasionally visiting the "French Opera" (where Adelina Patti[12] was then creating a furor by her first appearances), or witnessing the gorgeous pageant of Mardi Gras.

23

The political disputes which were beginning to darken the horizon of the country, and the mutterings of whose thunder were heard in the distance, at first distracted us but little from our ordinary pursuits. But as the storm gathered in darkness and violence we could not remain insensible to its influence. Without any disposition to violent partisanship, I had favored the party of which the standard-bearers were Bell and Everett[13] and the battle-cry "The Constitution and the Union," and I had grieved sincerely over its defeat by the Radicals of the North, aided by the "fire-eaters" of the South. Compton and Crain, if I remember rightly, were both members of the Breckenridge[14] wing of the Democratic party, but neither of them extreme in his views, and all of us were hopeful of, and indeed expected, some satisfactory compromise, which might at least tide over the difficulties of the political situation. Unfortunately, however, the violent men of both sides were in the ascendancy, and while the press of the North insultingly declared that "the South could not be kicked out of the Union," the southern press with equal folly asserted that "one Southerner could easily whip three Northerners" and dared the North to try coercion. Political madness ruled the hour.

The secession of South Carolina on December 20th, 1860, dissolved all illusions as to the tendencies of the future, and sent throughout the entire country a wave of excitement and agitation, such as it has never, before or since, been my fortune to witness. All business came to a standstill. Nothing was talked of but the political situation, and mass-meetings usurped the place of all ordinary occupations. Excitement ran wild, and I shall never forget a sermon in behalf of the "Union" preached by the Rev. Dr. Leacock of New Orleans, and which so offended a number of his audience that they arose at once from their seats and left the Church. A Union speech of Randall Hunt of New Orleans, made to an enormous assembly of citizens in Canal St. and greeted with the wildest cheers, stirred my rather unemotional soul to its lowest depths, and I remember my surprise at finding myself standing with my hat in my hand, waving and cheering with almost insane enthusiasm.

So far as my own observation and recollection can guide me, I should say now that a decided majority of the people of Louisiana were averse to secession and in favor of some compromise which might preserve their own threatened rights *within* the Union. But, like most conservatives, this major-

24

ity was timid and halting and without any leader, while the party of secession was in desperate earnest, thoroughly organized and led by active men in whom they had every confidence. The result may be readily imagined. Louisiana, by her Legislature and following the example of South Carolina, Mississippi, Florida, Alabama and Georgia, passed an ordinance of secession January 26th, 1861, an act received with the wildest evidences of delight by the secessionists, and with grief, doubt and dismay by the conservatives.

I was still in New Orleans when the ordinance of secession was passed, and do not remember that it disturbed materially the course of my studies. In fact, so far as I can recollect, the passage of this political Rubicon seemed to rather allay the preceding intensity of excitement. The die was cast, and all parties remained hushed in expectation of the next act of the great drama. I remember that I was still in New Orleans on Shrove Tuesday, February 12th, 1861, and witnessed the annual Mardi Gras festivities, with the torch-light pageant and procession of "The Mystic Crewe of Comus," which, on this occasion, if my memory does not mislead me, represented the "Seven Ages of Man."

RETURN TO ALEXANDRIA

Soon after, however, I must have returned to Alexandria, where I remained for a short time in the family of General G. Mason Graham The latter gentleman, whom I had already met in Tennessee, learning that I expected shortly to return to Alexandria and that I had no engagement, most kindly met me on the steamer at New Orleans and invited me to make my home with his family until his own return from Virginia, whither he was called by the exigencies of the political situation. This kind invitation relieved me of considerable embarrassment, as I preferred not to return to Mr. Compton's as a perhaps somewhat burdensome visitor and for an indefinite period, while my expenses in New Orleans had about exhausted my ready money. Accordingly I gladly accepted Gen. Graham's offer, and, on arriving in Alexandria went for a few days as a visitor to Mr. Compton's, and thence to the plantation of Gen. Graham, some five miles further up the Bayou Rapides.

Gen. Graham, a Virginian by birth, had acquired his military title in the Mexican War, and, though somewhat austere and precise in his manners, was a man of sterling worth and highly esteemed by his neighbors. At this period he was a widower, and his family, consisting of two sons, Donald and Duncan, and a daughter Amy, was directed by his sister, a widow, Mrs. Mason, who had been a warm friend and patron of mine in Tennessee. She was a lady of about forty years, possessing still traces of former beauty, somewhat stiff and precise in her manners, like her brother, the General, whom she almost worshipped. Both Gen. Graham and Mrs. Mason were enthusiasts relative to Virginia and Virginians, a characteristic which sometimes displayed itself rather amusingly, particularly in Mrs. Mason. The latter lady received me with cordiality and at once installed me as a sort of quasi-head to the family during the absence of Gen. Graham. The children, who had been under my instruction for a short time in Tennessee, read French with me, and we rode together often over the plantation.

Among the professors at the State Military Academy were two young Virginians, Major Smith and Dr. Powhatan Clark, both gay, rollicking young fellows, fond of society, entertaining talkers and of course "the rage" in the somewhat dull society circles of a small inland town. Naturally it was the correct thing for all the planters, and especially for those possessed of marriageable daughters, to invite the gay young professors to dinner, and I presume a Saturday or Sunday rarely passed on which this happy pair of inseparables did not enjoy some entertainment of this kind. As Virginians, Mrs. Mason, of course felt a warm interest in the young men, and in due course of time they were invited to dine with her. As the sole male adult of the family at this time I was called upon to act in a certain degree as their host, a position which my education and surroundings thus far had but poorly fitted me to fill, and between the somewhat severe and antique courtesy of Mrs. Mason, and the rather exuberant vivacity of the professors I felt greatly embarrassed, and was thoroughly conscious that I was not presenting myself in a favorable light.

Of course at the dinner table the conversation turned upon the burning subject of the right of secession and the political future of the country. Mrs. Mason was a warm Unionist and insisted that Virginia would *never, never,* prove so traitorous as to countenance the destruction of the Union. Dr. Clark was a hot-headed and blind partisan of secession, while Prof. Smith, though inclining to support his colleague, was more sober and thoughtful in his views, or perhaps more polite in declining to dispute the earnestness of his hostess. I had taken no special share in the conversation, though an interested listener, when suddenly Prof. Smith turned sharply towards me and enquired what were my views on the subject of secession. Startled somewhat by the unexpectedness of the question, which, indeed, I had never considered very carefully, and upon which I had formulated no very decided opinion, I stammered out that my mind was not as yet made up—a reply which thoroughly disgusted the good Mrs. Mason and elicited from her the warm rebuke: "Oh, do not say that! Do not be undecided in such a cause!" Poor Mrs. Mason! Virginia *did* countenance secession, and I have never known whether her love for the Union yielded to her state pride, or whether she continued a sincere and undisguised partisan of the Union to the close of the strife. So far as I know, however, Gen. Graham took no active part in the war. Prof. Smith was killed[15] near the close of the struggle in Virginia, and of Dr. Clark I have heard nothing since the dinner to which I have referred.[16]

Soon after this event I was invited to take charge of the education of the children of Mr. J. Routh Williams,[17] a sugar-planter residing some six or eight miles south of Alexandria. Mr. Williams was a jovial and hearty man of about forty-five years, devoted to the care of his plantation and yet fond of his family, for whom however the engrossing duties of his position left him comparatively little leisure. His family consisted of his wife, a noble and motherly woman who soon became almost a mother to me, and three children, two boys, Archie and Routh, aged about ten and twelve years, and a little girl of three or four. The boys were, of course, my especial charge, and a more high-spirited and unruly pair of colts it never fell to my lot to tame. However, there was nothing mean about them, and a few weeks of pretty rigid discipline reduced the boys to a pair of as fine, manly little fellows as one would wish to see. The parents were, of course, delighted with my success and made everything as agreeable to me as possible, so that I was perfectly satisfied with my position.

PREPARATION FOR WAR

Meanwhile, however, political affairs were hastening forward to the inevitable rupture, and the land was filled with excitement and rumors of impending war. The bombardment of Fort Sumter, April 12th, 1861, followed by the call of President Lincoln for 75,000 troops to suppress the "rebellion" and the secession of Virginia, April 17th, placed the two sections of the country face to face in the attitude of enemies. Throughout the broad surface of the entire land the roll of the drum and the cheers of the gathering volunteers drowned all other sounds, and all business was paralyzed before the pressure of the impending struggle, whose desperateness and magnitude however, neither President nor peasant realized. About this period I joined a company of so-called "home-guards" forming in my neighborhood, and whose duty it was to maintain order among the Negroes and other suspicious characters of the vicinity. This company, consisting chiefly of planters and their sons, met once or twice a week for drill, armed with shotguns or other private weapons. Our regular drill-master was a young planter, who by some chance had acquired a slight knowledge of the "Manual of Arms," and I remember well the hearty laugh we enjoyed at his expense, when, in his nervousness at the novelty of his position, he directed us to grasp our arms "two inches below the stock (lock)!"

About the first of June, Leroy A. Stafford, a cotton-planter of lower Red River, who had set to work to organize a company of volunteers for the impending war, dined at the house of his old friend Mr. Williams, and of course the threatened struggle formed the chief subject of conversation. Before leaving, Mr. Stafford, without directly asking me to join his company, intimated that he would be glad to have me do so, an intimation to which I made no definite reply at the time, but which occasioned me much reflection.

It seemed evident that a crisis had arrived in which it became necessary for every man to decide definitely upon his future course. Born and educated in the North, I did not share in any degree the fears of the Southerners over the election to the Presidency of Mr. Lincoln. I could not but think the action of the seceding States unwise and dangerous to their future prosperity. On the other hand, this action had already been taken, and without any prospect of its revocation. Indeed, in the present frame of mind of the North, any steps toward recession seemed likely to precipitate the very evils which the secession of the States had been designed to anticipate. I believed slavery a disadvantage to the South, but no *sin,* and, in any event, an institution for which the Southerners of the present day were not responsible. An inheritance from their forefathers, properly administered it was by no means an unmitigated evil, and it was one, moreover, in which the North but a few years before had shared. All my interests, present and future, apparently lay in the South and with Southerners, and if the seceding States, in one of which I resided, chose deliberately to try the experiment of self-government, I felt quite willing to give them such aid as lay in my feeble power. When I add to this that I was 24 years of age, and naturally affected largely by the ideas, the enthusiasm and the excitement of my surroundings, it is easy to understand to what conclusions I was led. A package of letters[18] written by me to my father during the war and carefully kept by him has been preserved to this day, and the letter numbered "I,"[19] written from New Orleans while en route to Camp Moore, will give a fair idea of my views at that period, and my reasons for volunteering in the Confederate Army.

Thus it came about that on Monday, June 17th, 1861, I enrolled my name as a private in the "Stafford Guards," as the company of Captain Stafford was then called. Returning quietly to my usual duties on the plantation, I said nothing of my action. But at the next meal Mr. Williams, who by chance had been into Alexandria that day, told his wife that I had volunteered, an announcement which led that good lady to burst into tears, and her example was followed by the two boys, my pupils, and, indeed, I feel quite sure that my own sight was somewhat dimmed for a moment by a few tears, which insisted on forcing themselves into prominence. No reproaches, however, were uttered by either Mr. or Mrs. Williams, and the latter, with true womanly instinct and forethought, set herself to work at once to put my wardrobe in good order for my departure. The next ten days were occupied in completing the organization of the company, a matter in which I took no part, never even appearing at the drills and musters. Thus it was not until about the last of June that, having bid a last farewell to all our friends, we hurried aboard the steamer for New Orleans. The trip was very hot and uncomfortable from the crowded condition of the steamer, and we were all glad enough to gain a sight of the steeples and towers of the Crescent City.

Our stay in the city, however, was very brief, and on Tuesday, July 2d., we took the cars for Camp Moore, a camp of instruction located about sixty miles above New Orleans on the railroad. Here we were fairly initiated into the mysteries and miseries of a soldier's life, though the miseries of this camp were bliss itself when compared with the more serious discomforts of our later experience. Still our want of familiarity with hardships of all kinds made the petty trials of our first camp seem very formidable. In Camp Moore I found my first opportunity of becoming acquainted with the organization and personnel of the company[20] in which I was to serve.

Our captain, L. A. Stafford, was a man of no special military ability and of no military education, fond of a glass of liquor, though very rarely drinking to excess, fond also of a friendly game of cards, affable and pleasant when unopposed, but violent and somewhat tyrannical when aroused by opposition. He proved himself a warm and sincere friend to me, and I am told one of his latest inquiries was as to my fate. Stafford was as brave a man as ever lived, but the unfortunate lack of a military education and experience always prevented any brilliant success on his part as a commander. Our first lieutenant whose name[21] has escaped my memory, was a quiet gentlemanly officer, of more than average ability, but whose delicate health compelled him to leave the service before we became thoroughly acquainted with him.

The second lieutenant, Cummings, was a brother of Lieutenant Commander A. B. Cummings of the U. S. Navy, an affable and pleasant companion, who also developed gradually into a good officer. Though a Northern man by birth, he sealed his devotion to the South with his life on the bloody field near Fredericksburg. The third lieutenant, Albert Bringhurst, was a rather selfish and conceited young man, who had had, I think, a partial military education in the State Military Academy, and who developed into a very good officer under the trials and exigencies of active service.[22] Finally our orderly sergeant was good Dave Workman, a young cadet from the State Military Academy, whose military education served an excellent purpose in initiating the raw and green material under his immediate charge into the routine of a soldier's life, and whose manly, handsome face, patience and imperturbable temper, made him the favorite of the entire command. Many of the rank and file were the sons of planters and acquaintances of mine, though I missed the face of my old and intimate friend, John Compton, who had promised to join us in New Orleans, but, alas, never made his appearance.

At Camp Moore we were united with other volunteer companies to form the 9th Regiment of Louisiana Volunteers, of which we formed Company "B."[23] Our colonel was "Dick" Taylor,[24] a son of "Old Zach," the President of the United States, and a man who subsequently acquired high rank and considerable fame in the Southern Confederacy, and who has written one of the most piquant and entertaining books on the war (*Destruction and Reconstruction*, D. Appleton and Co., New York, 1879). The lieutenant-colonel, Randolph, was an excellent disciplinarian and drill-master, and to him the regiment owed all its knowledge of tactics and the greater part of its efficiency. A rather reserved and studious man, he won our esteem by his thoroughness and equability of character, but was removed from command before our entry upon active service and too soon to witness the results of his conscientious and honest labors. The major, Walker, was a fat, good-natured, short-winded and red-faced officer, who had apparently seen some service, but whose tactical ability was apparently limited to two commands, viz.: "By the right of companies to the rear (he called it "rare") into column," and "Left into-line wheel," and under the direction of his stentorian voice the command "rared" into column for many hours each day during our sojourn at Camp Moore. Some of our experiences in this, our first camp, illustrate the peculiarities of raw volunteer troops and the miseries of the green soldier's life so well that a few incidents from our experiences may prove entertaining.

The "Stafford Guards," as I have already mentioned, consisted largely of the sons of well-to-do planters, with whom were associated a few "roughs," chiefly denizens of the "piney-woods" regions north of Alexandria, and perhaps half-a-dozen Jews, most of whom had carried a pack along the Red River. These Jews, singular as it may seem, proved themselves as faithful and efficient soldiers as any in the command, and shed their blood for the cause of the South as freely as the natives "to the manner born." The task of enforcing military discipline upon a collection of "young gentlemen," as most of us were, was by no means easy, and poor Dave Workman's youth and modesty made the duties of orderly sergeant particularly burdensome to him. We arrived at Camp Moore in the midst of a severe storm of rain, and, as our camp equipage had not yet arrived, were assigned for temporary quarters to an old barn, where, worn out by the novel experiences of the day, we rested our heads upon our knapsacks and slept promiscuously upon the floor. About midnight the train containing our equipage made its appearance, and an order was sent out to march a detail from the company to the station and unload our baggage. I shall never forget the anxious face of poor Workman as, by the dim light of a dirty lantern, he stumbled about among the heavy sleepers, making vain efforts to find and awaken the men whose initials upon the muster-roll rendered them liable to duty upon the first camp detail; nor the sigh of relief which arose from the fortunate volunteers whose names were *not* reached on the disagreeable list, as the heavy rain pattered down on the roof of our homely, but dry, quarters. The next day, however, was fair, and the regimental camping-ground was laid out in regular streets, tents were erected, cooking utensils distributed, and the regular course of camp life begun.

The following Sunday I arrayed myself in a clean suit, and, after breakfast, sat down in my tent to write some letters, when my serenity was disturbed by the appearance of the handsome face of Workman, who, in an apologetic tone of voice, informed me that, in consequence of the sickness of some of the men, he had been obliged to detail me for "police duty," and wished me to report at once at the captain's tent. I arose immediately with unabated cheerfulness and, assuring him of my readiness for duty at all times, proceeded to "report" at the place indicated. Here I found that I, with several "other" Irishmen, was assigned to the agreeable duty of carrying out of the camp grounds the company slops, a large barrel fairly running over with decaying meat and vegetables, and reeking with the vile odors of refuse of every variety. It was a disgusting job, but I was "soldiering" now in earnest, and, having put my hand to the plow, did not intend to look backwards. So we seized upon our disgusting burden, and with no little difficulty succeeded in conveying it outside of the camp limits and emptying it. Next we were assigned to the duty of "policing" the parade-ground, i.e., cleaning it of all brush, stones and other obstructions, which were carefully carried into one corner of the grounds one day, and with like ceremony carried back again to another corner by the detail of the following day. Of course this work was done to keep us busy and give us exercise, but at the time it seemed to us quite absurd.

JOURNEY TO VIRGINIA

Guard duty and frequent drills occupied most of our time and served to keep off homesickness until Thursday, July 11th, when the Ninth Regiment were packed like sardines in box and platform cars and started for Richmond, via Grand Junction, Chattanooga, Knoxville, Lynchburg &c. Some delay occurred at Grand Junction, and here, I think, was taken the picture in my original volunteer uniform, which was forwarded to my father in Tennessee, and, singularly enough, has survived the vicissitudes of almost a third of a century. Another delay at Knoxville gave us leisure to inspect that city, and particularly the home of "Parson Brownlow," whose violent expression of Union sentiments, in language often far more forcible than elegant, had won for him our cordial hatred. It was not until Wednesday, July 17th, that we reached Richmond, tired and dirty, and were marched out to the fair grounds, then known as "Camp Hermitage," and occupied as a camp of instruction. Here was written my letter numbered 2.[25]

Our stay in Richmond, however, was but brief, and on the evening of July 20th, while the air was filled with rumors of impending battle, we "double-quicked" to the railroad station, and, after innumerable and vexatious delays, finally succeeded in fairly getting off for Manassas Junction. But the delays which marked the beginning of our expedition hung about it until its close, and it was not until the early dawn of Monday, July 22d, that our command disembarked at the Junction, and for the first time we received news of the battle of the preceding day with its dear-bought victory. Filled with wonder we wandered about gazing upon the wounded and the prisoners collected at the R. R. station, and gradually acquiring a slight perception of the horrors of war.

The regiment was encamped at once near Manassas Junction, and the business of instruction in the art of war was resumed and pushed forward as rapidly as possible. It was soon discovered, however, that our camping-ground was far from healthy, and this fact, with the unavoidable hardships and irregularities of a soldier's life, soon increased enormously our sick-list. Typhoid fever and dysentery more than decimated our ranks, so that by the first of September we were fairly driven to change our quarters. Accordingly the regiment was moved forward to the vicinity of Centerville, where in "Camp Bienville" we enjoyed better water and improved health. Here too we were brigaded[26] with the 6th, 7th and 8th Louisiana regiments and "Wheat's Battalion" (commonly known as "the Tigers"), under the command of Brig. Gen'l. W. H. T. Walker[27] of Georgia, an officer educated at West Point and distinguished by much severe service in the Seminole and Mexican wars. Gen. Walker had been desperately wounded on several occasions, but recovered, as he said, "to spite the doctors," although the permanent evidences of his sufferings remained in a painfully spare frame and a pale cadaverous complexion, which always suggested a ghost on horseback.

WHEAT'S BATTALION

Mention has been made of "Wheat's Battalion," an organization which in course of time communicated the name of "Louisiana Tigers" to most of the troops from Louisiana engaged in the Army of Northern Virginia. It consisted of three companies, under the command of Major "Bob" Wheat,[28] the adventurous son of an Episcopal clergyman, who left school to join the army in the Mexican War. Following Lopez[29] to Cuba, he in some way escaped the garotte only to enlist under Walker[30] in his unfortunate expedition to Nicaragua. As Taylor says: "Exhausting the capacities of South American patriots to *pronounce*, he quitted their society in disgust and joined Garibaldi in Italy, whence his keen scent of combat summoned him home in convenient time to receive a bullet at Manassas. The most complete Dugald Dalgetty[31] possible, he had 'all the defects of the good qualities' of that doughty warrior.''[32] Of the three companies which composed Major Wheat's battalion, the largest and most disreputable bore the name of the "Louisiana Tigers," who are humorously, but quite justly, described in the following passage from Gen. Taylor's book already mentioned: "Recruited on the levee and in the alleys of New Orleans, the men might have come out of 'Alsatia,' where they would have been worthy subjects of that illustrious potentate 'Duke Hildebrod.'[33] The captain who had succeeded to the immediate command of these worthies on the advancement of Wheat, enjoying the luxury of many aliases, called himself White, perhaps out of respect for the purity of the patriotic garb lately assumed. So villainous was the reputation of this battalion that every commander desired to be rid of it, and General Johnston assigned it to me, despite my efforts to decline the honor of such society.''[34]

Considerably to our horror, in the formation of the brigade encampment, Wheat's Battalion, was located immediately next to the 9th Louisiana Regiment, and, indeed, just alongside of my company. Yet, singular as it may seem, we never had the slightest difficulty with them, and in fact the regiment and battalion got along together so well that they were often jestingly called "the happy family."

Of course in such a command as "the Tigers" ludicrous incidents were of frequent occurrence. I remember, for instance, that on cold and frosty mornings the orderly sergeant of this model company contented himself with merely poking his head out of his tent and calling the roll, the men in like manner answering from the warm shelter of their blankets. It was said too that this sergeant, a New Orleans prize-fighter, some six and a half feet in height, was in the habit once a month of calling "the Tigers" into line, removing his coat with much ceremony, and then addressing his comrades as follows: "Now men, yez have seen me lay down me sthripes. If any of yez has anything agin me let him step out like a man and settle it with me." This cheerful and manly invitation, accompanied by the exhibition of an arm of extraordinary muscular development, rarely succeeded in awakening much enthusiasm in his command, and if any grudges existed they seem to have been nipped in the bud. Major Wheat and Captain Stafford became warm friends, and in this way we saw quite a little of the renowned fillibuster[35] [sic] and free-lance. It was from this "Camp Bienville" that my letter numbered "3" was written,[36] and about this time Capt. Stafford appointed me the accountant and bookkeeper of his company, a position

34

which relieved me from much of the drudgery of camp life, and which I continued to hold until detailed for special duty in the Quartermaster's Department.

TYPHOID FEVER

About October 1st of this year I came down with typhoid fever and was ordered to hospital at Charlottesville. The chaplain of our regiment, Rev. Caleb Dowe, who had been the rector of our parish in Alexandria, most kindly volunteered to accompany me to Charlottesville, and actually did take me to Gordonsville, where I obstinately persisted in disembarking and positively refused to proceed any further. A comrade, William Bush, who had been attacked with dysentery some month or two before, had in some way landed upon the farm of Mr. James Newman, a well-to-do planter located some five or six miles from Gordonsville, and had written such attractive stories of the hospitality and kindness of his host that they had impressed themselves firmly upon my mind. Accordingly, on arriving in Gordonsville, I insisted that Mr. Dowe should write to Mr. Newman, asking him to send in his carriage for me and take me to his home until my recovery. I am surprised now at my own impudence in thus forcing myself on Mr. Newman's hospitality, and can ascribe it to nothing but the delirious recklessness of a very sick man: but the generous kindness of my host, a noble specimen of a true Virginia gentleman, was equal to the occasion, and without further question he sent his colored man and carriage for me the next day. I was assisted into the carriage by Mr. Dowe, who then bade me adieu, and after a ride which utterly exhausted my little remaining strength, I remember my arrival at Mr. Newman's house, and that I was picked up from the bottom of the carriage, where I had fallen, and carefully placed in bed.

The succeeding three weeks of my life are a complete blank, or rather seem like a troubled dream, and my first clear recollection of subsequent events begins with the appearance at my bedside of a middle-aged lady, of kindly face, who carefully bathed my face and hands in cold water and asked me how I felt. The fever had left me, but I was weak as a child and entirely unable to help myself. Soon after I recognized the familiar face of my friend Bush and learned that I had been very ill with typhoid fever and owed my life, under God, to the kind care of Mrs. Newman and professional ministrations of the good Dr. Jones,[37] of Orange Co., Virginia. Mr. Newman had fitted up two of his Negro-cabins as hospitals, and with the aid of Dr. Jones had nursed and fed a large number of sick Confederate soldiers, without money and without price—a pure and noble Christian beneficence which we poor invalids could reward only with our gratitude and our prayers.

My convalescence was slow, or at least seemed so to my impatience, and my letter numbered "4" and dated Oct. 29th, 1861,[38] was about the first-fruits of my returning strength. However, the kindness of my host and hostess proved equal to the tediousness of my recovery, and a short time before Christmas I was able to bid them adieu and to return to camp near Centerville. Here I found some changes in the organization of my command, Col. Taylor having been promoted to Brigadier General, and Lt. Col. Randolph having assumed the rank and title of a full colonel. Soon after we removed our camp to a position east of Manassas Junction, and proceeded to build winter-quarters in the shape of rough but comfortable log-cabins. From the burden of this rather severe labor I was relieved by my position as company bookkeeper, which not only protected me from much drudgery but also furnished me with congenial employment.

CHRISTMAS 1861

Our Christmas of this year I shall never forget. In the absence of my mess-mates, who were engaged in felling timber for our winter cabin, I volunteered to provide and cook our Christmas dinner. After a long and earnest search I succeeded in securing a hen, whose mature years and general gravity of demeanor merited a better fate, together with a canteen of bad corn-whiskey, which exhaled ambrosial odors to our unaccustomed senses. On Xmas Eve, after smoking our pipes and exchanging experiences and reminiscences before a huge fire of logs, my messmates and I "turned in" into our tent to sleep the sleep of the just and the weary, I having previously tethered the fowl of many hopes by her leg to one of the pins of the tent, and placed the precious canteen beneath my pillow-knapsack.

My well-earned slumbers were rudely disturbed at some uncertain hour of the night by an unearthly shriek and a sudden feeling of suffocation, which led me to paw wildly with both hands and feet, until, removing from my face the obstructing burden which was smothering me, I caught a glimpse by the starlight of my gallinaceous prize fluttering in mid air and

36

uttering squawk after squawk of unmitigated terror. Jumping up hastily with my companions, scarcely comprehending what had occurred, we gazed at each other for a moment in blank amazement. The ludicrousness of the situation, however, soon burst upon us. The sportive breezes of midnight uniting their efforts into a small cyclone, had borne down upon our camp, and seizing playfully the corner of our tent had ripped up the pegs which confined its corners, flung our sleeping Christmas dinner wildly into the air, and precipitated the entire structure upon its unconscious inmates. With a shout of laughter we rushed to the rescue, captured the hysterical fowl, whose tether fortunately had not broken, and after some trouble succeeded in erecting once more our frail shelter. In a few moments we were again all sleeping soundly, and reveille alone restored us to consciousness and the brightness of Christmas Day.

But alas! as I arose from my warm blankets an aromatic and delectable odor diffused itself through the tent, and hastily rummaging for the canteen I found it safely nestled near my feet, but *minus the cork,* which had been displaced during the confusion of our nocturnal adventure and more than half the precious spirits had bathed our unappreciative blankets. But spilled whiskey is like spilled milk, and with sad and chastened spirits we prepared for the duties of the day. With some prevision that my Christmas fowl might prove in truth a genuine *pièce de résistance,* I proceeded early to wring her neck, and soon had her cooking in a skillet over a lovely bed of coals. But the longer she cooked, the larger and tougher she seemed to get, and by the time my messmates returned from their labors she presented the appearance of a small turkey and resisted probing with the fork like the seat of an English saddle. My comrades laughed and joked at my embarrassment and congratulated me upon the *satisfying* character of my provisions, but hard work and easy consciences supplied good appetites, and we tore the old hen to pieces and devoured her, skin and all, with genuine Christmas hilarity.

PICKET DUTY

On January 21st, 1862,[39] we were ordered upon our first tour of picket duty for six days on the line of the Occoquan River, some six or eight miles from camp. Though my official duties exempted me from this service, I felt anxious to see some active military life, and accordingly accompanied

37

my command to the position assigned. On arriving at our destination the regiment was divided into details and assigned to various posts to watch and guard the different roads traversing the neighborhood. My company was stationed in a wood, and a small detail of eight or ten men with a corporal was placed on a wooded hill some half a mile from the reserve. My tour on post came about midnight, and at the designated hour the corporal escorted me with the relief to my post, where I received from my predecessor the few instructions committed to him, and was then left to my own devices.

The night was cloudy, and the trees rendered the vicinity as dark as Egypt, but, as my eyes became accustomed to the gloom, I was able to distinguish a narrow wood-road leading down apparently into a dark gulf, at the head of which my post was situated. The novelty of the situation of course put my nerves somewhat upon the stretch, and as I listened with all my ears to detect any sounds of life in the gulf below, I busied myself with conjectures as to what I ought to do under these or those conditions, equally averse to earning the laughter of my comrades by an unnecessary alarm, or allowing them to incur surprise and danger by remissness of duty on my part. As time stole by, however, and no cause for alarm presented itself, the stillness and monotony of my surroundings began to render me drowsy, when, on a sudden, a weird and unearthly noise from the depths of the dark gulf roused me with a sudden start, and I stood straining my very eyeballs into the gloom, in the effort to see the cause of this horrible clamor. Another unearthly shriek, and this time manifestly nearer than before, made my very hair stand on end. I hastily cocked my gun, sprung behind a tree, and, I doubt not, would have fired at once upon any person or thing which chanced to make its appearance at that moment. But for a few moments all was quiet as the grave. Not even a leaf seemed to rustle upon my strained senses. Then the same unearthly cry recurred, but this time evidently more remote and far off to my right, and, as reason once more resumed her sway, I recognized the weird voice of the screech-owl, as he flitted along the line of our pickets. With a long breath of relief I uncocked my gun, but no further drowsiness benumbed my thoroughly awakened senses, and it is needless to say that I was thoroughly happy when the approach of the relief enabled me to return to the camp-fire of the reserve and the companionship of my comrades. The next day I joined heartily in the laugh at a comrade, who was said to have fled from his post at the cry of an owl the preceding night, but I carefully kept my own counsel.

38

SPRING RAINS

At the expiration of our tour of duty[40] we returned to camp, and the winter wore away in our quarters without any considerable excitement. As, however, the fair weather of Spring began to appear, evidences of moving became manifest and the camp was filled with rumors, extravagant and contradictory. At last, on Saturday, March 8th, 1862, we were ordered to pack our baggage at once and be ready to move on the morrow. Of course the accretions of the winter had filled our cabins with numerous little conveniences which it was absolutely necessary to discard, but the duty of selection was sad and difficult. On Sunday, however, we all appeared in line with huge knapsacks strapped upon our backs and various unmilitary appendages about us, accessories which the experience of the next few days taught us to discard with disgust. The cabins in which we had enjoyed so much comfort were committed to the flames, and with excited but saddened hearts we turned our faces southward and proceeded, via Brentsville, to the Rappahannock River, which we crossed on March 11th, by the bridge of the Orange and Alexandria Railroad.

The rain had fallen almost incessantly during our march, and our camps along the Rappahannock were converted into shallow lakes by the standing water, which prevented comfortable rest by night or day. After a week or more of such experience, thoroughly worn out by want of sleep, I determined one rainy evening to slip quietly out of camp and seek some shelter where I might rest comfortably for one night at least. Accordingly soon after sunset I stole away in the drizzling gloom, and avoiding the sentinels wandered off at hazard in search of shelter. After a walk of perhaps half an hour I descried upon a hill a short distance from me an old church, which seemed to offer protection from the increasing storm, and hastening my steps toward it I was both surprised and somewhat startled as I drew near to observe through the windows the reflection of lights which indicated that the building was already inhabited. However, we have the testimony of Horace that *Vacuus viator cantabit coram latrone,*[41] and I felt desperate enough to face almost anything for the chance of securing shelter.

Opening the door carefully and peering within, a novel sight met my eye. Most of the pews were already occupied by soldiers who had fled to the sacred building for shelter, each of them having preempted his own position and spread his blanket upon the seat. A large fire had been started in the stove, upon the surface of which numerous slices of bacon were cooking and diffusing an appetizing odor throughout the building. Some were eating their suppers, some smoking and chatting together, while others had already yielded to sleep. The high, old-fashioned pulpit was occupied by a New Orleans prize-fighter, Tom Jennings, whose face was familiar among the "Tigers," and his legs hung gracefully over the sides as he lounged upon the seat and smoked his pipe with an air of solid comfort and unqualified satisfaction. Stealing quietly to a vacant pew near the rear of the church, I ate my frugal supper and in turn drew forth my pipe and amused myself by watching the scene.

Most of my neighbors, having now finished their meal and betaken themselves to their pews and their pipes, the hum of conversation and the sharp jokes and repartee of men of little refinement, but thoroughly good-natured and happy, re-echoed from side to side and occasioned outbursts of hearty laughter. Gradually songs of a familiar kind were heard, and the chorus was taken up by numerous voices until the very rafters resounded with the noisy strains. After a time a vulgar song was sung by some soldier, and received with such laughter that his example seemed on the point of being followed by others, when I was thoroughly surprised to see Tom Jennings rise in the pulpit and address the riotous assembly in the following words: "See here boys! I am just as bad as any of you, I know. But this is a church and I'll be damned if it's right to sing any of your smutty songs in here, and it's got to be stopped." It *was* stopped too. Either tender consciences or Tom's reputation and influence was effective at once, and soon we all dropped off to sleep. Poor Tom Jennings! When next I saw him he was borne off the field of Cold Harbor, writhing with agony from a gunshot wound through the bowels and pale with the pallor of approaching death. I hope the recording angel jotted down poor Tom's protest against obscenity in the little church upon the Rappahannock, and that the entry blotted out many pages of vice and sin.

SHENANDOAH VALLEY CAMPAIGN[42]

In the morning, refreshed and strengthened by a comfortable night's rest, I returned to my command, where, so far as I know, I had not been missed. Towards the close of April we moved from the vicinity of Brandy Station, via Gordonsville, Stanardsville and Swift Run Gap to the Shenandoah Valley, and camped on Wednesday, April 30th, 1862, near

40

Conrad's Store. Our brigade, commanded by Gen. "Dick" Taylor, consisted at this period of the 5th, 6th, 7th, 8th and 9th[43] Louisiana regiments with Wheat's Battalion, and formed with the brigades of Gen. Geo. H. Stewart, Gen. Arnold Elzey and Gen. Trimble the division of Major General Richard S. Ewell.[44] We remained encamped near Conrad's Store for nearly a month, the monotony of camp life disturbed only by a slight skirmish on a peak of the Massanutten range of mountains, which begins here to divide the Shenandoah Valley into two parts. It chanced that this skirmish was borne by my company, which was on picket duty at this station, and I remember well my chagrin that I was absent from this first baptism of my command with fire, and the haste with which I baked some unleavened biscuit for rations and started at once for the scene of action on the arrival of the exciting news. Of course the affair was over long before I reached the picket post, but I heartily enjoyed the various stories of the encounter and the enchanting views of Harrisonburg and the valley which rewarded my enthusiasm.

On May 21st, after a rather hard march, we joined the command of Major General Thomas J. Jackson (the redoubtable "Stonewall") near Newmarket, and, leaving the valley "pike," turned sharply to the east, crossed the Massanutten range to Luray and then bore north again along the eastern bank of the Shenandoah toward Front Royal. This latter town we struck about 2 P.M. on Friday, May 23d, and here for the first time I heard the hostile whistle of shell and Minié ball.[45] The First Maryland (Federal) regiment, commanded by Col. Kenly,[46] occupied the town, and, though both surprised by our approach and greatly outnumbered, made for a few moments an active and honorable resistance. Our numbers, however, were so superior that a hasty rush, a volley or two of musketry, and the battle was over, the fugitive enemy hastening away towards Winchester with our cavalry in hot pursuit. I think on this occasion I fired two rounds, one at a small body of the enemy in the woods, and another at a man racing away along the railroad track and at least half a mile from me. At the report of my gun the latter gave a few extra leaps and disappeared behind the embankment. He was unquestionably too far off to be hurt, but it is just possible he may have heard the whistle of my bullet. As we passed through the town I saw my first dead enemy, a large, muscular man, in the uniform of a private, lying just at the gate of a private house.

Encamping for the night just beyond the town, the next day (Saturday) we left the main road to Winchester at Cedarville, and, taking a rather obscure wood-road to the left, advanced cautiously towards Middletown on the valley pike. We reached this point about 2 P.M., striking the rear of Gen. Banks's[47] column in full retreat from Strasburg. The pike was filled with a column of cavalry, who, as we made our unwelcome appearance, rode madly along the road in the direction of Winchester in order to pass the point of danger. Hemmed in between two high stone fences, they could make but little resistance, and furnished an excellent target for our infantry, though in a few moments the dust hid all distinct forms from our sight. Quite a number were killed and wounded, though not nearly so many as one might reasonably expect. Banks's line, however, was cut in two, his rear guard being separated from the remainder of the column and driven back to Strasburg. As we jumped over the stone wall into the pike, however, a vicious volley of bullets whistled through our disordered ranks, splintering the rails of the neighboring fence and wounding several of my comrades, and, looking down the road towards Strasburg, I saw a company of Zouaves (Collis's)[48] behind a stone wall firing vigorously upon our advance. Hastily leaving the open pike, we rushed forward under the protection of the houses and fences until, emerging from the southern end of the village, we found our enemies in rapid retreat. After a short halt to reform our ranks, we again advanced in skirmish line to find the enemy, but on reaching Cedar Creek were ordered to retrace our steps. The excitement of the battle had begun to wear off, and we soon felt the fatigue and hunger of men who had been marching all day with little or no food.

Yet our orders were to press forward to Winchester, distant some thirteen miles, and footsore and faint, we struggled forward until late in the night, when fairly worn out we bivouacked by the roadside and snatched a few hours of sorely needed rest. As the sun rose in the morning we too arose from the ground and, stiff and sore, pushed on towards Winchester, where the roar of cannon and rattle of musketry indicated the existence of a sharp struggle. But we were too late to participate in the battle in which the remainder of Taylor's brigade bore so noble a part,[49] and in truth were not sorry to join with our comrades in a well-earned rest.

Camping near Winchester for a day or two, we then moved down to the vicinity of Halltown, but news of the approach of the converging columns of Frémont and Shields[50] upon our line of retreat indicated the necessity of the utmost rapidity of movement, and on Saturday, May 31st, we retreated from Halltown to the vicinity of Strasburg, some thirty miles, without rest. On our arrival at Middletown I slipped quietly into the house of a villager whose acquaintance I had made on our first hurried visit to this place and was greeted with a hot supper of excellent quality and a comfortable bed, luxuries which I had not enjoyed for many months. In the morning, after a hearty breakfast, I rejoined my command which had bivouacked some two miles beyond Middletown, and moved forward with them to Strasburg, luckily escaping the cavalry of Gen. Shields which entered Middletown about half an hour after I left and captured quite a number of stragglers.

Sunday, June 1st, 1862, we spent facing Frémont on the hills west of Strasburg, holding him in check while our immense train of captured supplies was making its way up the valley pike. Sunday night we also retired, forming the rear guard of the army and harassed from time to time by Frémont's cavalry. By the 3rd we reached Mount Jackson, and by the 5th Harrisonburg, where leaving the valley pike we turned in a south-east direction toward Port Republic and Brown's Gap.

At this point, thoroughly worn out by hard marching and loss of sleep, I decided to take refuge in the quartermaster's department, where I had been detailed as a clerk about a month before. The precise location of the regimental train was, however, rather uncertain, and having lost my way in the search for it I suffered severely from lack of food, supporting myself by corn stolen from the horses of other trains until I succeeded in finding that of my own regiment shortly after the battles of Cross Keys and Port Republic.[51] Of course, therefore, I did not participate in either of these battles, so bloody and so glorious to the Confederate arms.

From June 12th to June 17th we were encamped near Weyer's Cave, where we enjoyed the luxuries of a good bath, an abundance of food, clean clothes and the rest which we all so much needed. On June 17th, however, we started for Richmond via Charlottesville, Gordonsville, Louisa Court House, etc., to Ashland, where we arrived on June 25th. This movement, which was made partly by marching and partly by the cars, was for several days shrouded in mystery even to our own officers, while the country was filled with all sorts of contradictory rumors relative to our destination and objects. It was not until we reached Ashland that the real purpose of the movement became apparent.

The prospect of renewed fighting here again induced me to shoulder my musket and rejoin my command, and early on the morning of June 26th we left Ashland and plunged into the woods and swamps bordering upon the Chickahominy River. The sound of artillery upon our right indicated that the ball had already opened, but we met no enemy during this day and bivouacked at night near Hundley's Corners, every man in his position in the ranks with his gun beside him. How long we had slept thus I have no means of determining, but I was suddenly awakened by the most unearthly and terrible shriek that ever greeted mortal ears. It seemed too that every man in the division was aroused by the same cry, and though the darkness was such that my nearest neighbor was invisible, the rustle of clothing and the sharp rattle of arms told me that every man was starting to his feet at the same instant. Springing hastily behind a tree just at hand, I involuntarily cocked my gun, and I feel quite certain that in my dazed condition I should have fired upon anyone, friend or foe, who might have approached me. A moment of intense suspense followed, in which the smothered command "Fall in Company C" rather alarmed than reassured me as it sounded in rear of me. Another moment and reason reasserted her sway. Observing no further portent of danger, comrade called quietly to comrade to inquire what was the matter, and the voices of men speaking in stern tones to horses soon suggested to our strained senses the solution of the alarm. Col. Stafford (our captain had been promoted to the colonelcy of our regiment early in the Spring) rode a magnificent chestnut stallion, and the Lieut. Col., Peck, was likewise the possessor of a tremendous coal-black stallion of great power. In picketing the horses for the night the servants had been careless, and one of the horses breaking loose had at once attacked the other. It was the agonizing cry of one of these beasts which had so nearly stampeded the slumbering division. With muttered curses upon the restless brutes we lay down again to rest and slept the sleep of the weary until the dawn recalled us to the trials of a soldier's life.

Snatching a hasty breakfast we once more began our advance, and during almost the whole day marched through and by deserted camps strewn with the débris of our departed foes. Thousands upon thousands of letters were scattered over the ground, and for hours as we marched slowly and cautiously forward we amused ourselves with reading these records of private life and relations. Many of the letters which fell under my eye were ad-

44

dressed to volunteers from the Eastern States, and I remember my astonishment at the numerous errors in spelling which defaced epistles characterized by excellent chirography and correct and even elegant modes of expression. Manifestly the education of many of the writers had been superficial and showy, rather than thoroughly grounded in the rudiments.

About two o'clock frequent halts and the rattle of musketry at no great distance warned us that sterner duties were at hand. Col. Stafford and Major Wheat rode together at the head of our regiment, and I remember well the subdued and almost sad manner of the famous soldier of fortune as he spoke of his past life and future prospects, and recalled reminiscences of his mother and early acquaintances. It surprised me to see so much genuine and deep feeling in one who bore the reputation of utter insensibility to the finer relations of life.

Soon the whistle of an occasional shell bade us prepare for action, and after some delay and apparent hesitation we formed in line of battle and advanced across an open field and through a marshy stream about knee-deep into a tangled wood which apparently covered a hill before us. Here again the direction of our advance seemed uncertain, while no enemy was visible, though the occasional whiz of a bullet assured us that the foe was not far distant. Finally obliquing somewhat to the right we ascended in rather broken order a slight ridge in the forest, when a perfect hailstorm of bullets greeted our advance. Still no enemy was to be seen, and the rattle of musketry, whiz of Minié balls and fall of the killed and wounded alone assured us that the foe was before us.

Now was the critical moment when a voice of authority to guide our uncertain steps and a bold officer to lead us forward would have been worth to us a victory. But none such appeared. Gen. Taylor was sick and absent. The gallant Col. Seymour who commanded in his absence had already fallen, while Col. Stafford who succeeded to the command by right of seniority, had not heard of his death.[53] The line paused in natural hesitation and began firing almost at random or at the smoke which now eddied through the trees. I peered vainly through the dense undergrowth to find some target worthy of my aim. At last, in despair of seeing the enemy in my present position, I knelt down in order to look beneath the bushes, and as I did so felt my hat (a tall felt cavalry hat picked up on the field at Middletown) tipped upon my head as I supposed by an overhanging twig. My change of position was rewarded by the sight of a man firing from behind a large pine tree, perhaps sixty yards in our front, and sighting hastily along my barrel

I fired. A shower of bark from the trunk of the tree told me that I had missed my man and I hastened to reload for another trial.

Just then, a little to my left and perhaps ten paces in advance of our line, I noticed Major Wheat picking his way slowly and carefully through the dense underbrush, quiet and determined apparently, but uttering no word and followed by none of his own, or, indeed, any other command. A moment more and he fell motionless, seemingly without a groan or struggle, and I knew that his restless career was ended.[54] At the same time a comrade just to my left fell with a groan and turned upon me a beseeching look which I could not resist. Stepping hastily back to Capt. Cummings, I asked permission to remove my friend from the fatal crest of the hill to a lower position in [the] rear, and as with another comrade I stooped to pick him up, my assistant himself fell beside us both, another victim of the murderous fire of our unseen enemies. Calling to still another comrade for aid, we succeeded in dragging my wounded friend behind the exposed crest, where I was about to leave him to return to my position when the whole line retreated slowly down the hill to where I was, apparently dazed rather than alarmed, uncertain what to do and abandoning almost mechanically a hopeless position where no one seemed competent to direct them.

At this moment with a shout and a rush appeared the brigade of Hood's gallant Texans[55] sweeping by and over us and disappearing like a vision in the underbrush and the smoke. One deafening yell, one rattling volley and the victory was won. As we withdrew into the open field to reform our shattered ranks I saw poor Tom Jennings borne by, pale and groaning, and the recollection of his noble stand for principle in the little church on the Rappahannock flashed vividly across my recollection. *Requiescat in pace.*

Such was the [first] battle of Cold Harbor [1862, usually called Gaines' Mill] as it met my view. The attack of my command had proved a complete failure, not from any deficiency in the mettle of the men, but simply from the absence of all guidance and direction. Ignorant of the position of the enemy and consequently of what they were expected to do, they simply halted and wasted their lives and their blood in awaiting the command which never came. As the sun sank below the horizon our reformed brigade pushed forward again over the crest of the hill now wrested from the enemy, and for the first time had an idea of the position before which they had wasted their strength in a vain fusillade. A plateau of considerable extent spread out upon the summit of the hill, the crest and sides of which were covered with trees and undergrowth. Just at the brow of the hill a breastwork of logs, perhaps waist-high, formed a formidable fortification, protecting as well as concealing its defenders. It was from this line of works that our hidden enemies had poured upon us their deadly fire. To halt before such a volcano was madness. The only hope was to storm it rapidly, and this the gallant Texans under their bold leader happily accomplished.

Bivouacking upon the field of battle for the night, we proceeded the next day to Dispatch Station on the York River railroad, advancing again slowly as if uncertain what we might find in our front. No enemy however, appeared, and we turned to retrace our steps to one of the lower bridges of the Chickahominy, in order to cross to the south side of that river. The day was hot, our progress slow, and about 2 P.M. a halt enabled me to snatch a hasty dinner of crackers and raw pork, after which I seated myself upon a log at the foot of a dead and dry tree and fell fast asleep. A crash as if the very heavens had opened brought me suddenly to my feet, while the dry limbs of the tree beneath which I was sitting rattled about me like drops of rain in a heavy shower. I sprang into the narrow road with my comrades, and again rushed back hastily into the woods to escape a couple of ambulances, whose horses, terrified by the tremendous explosion, tore down the narrow way in reckless fright. In a few moments Gen. Ewell and staff galloped hastily by towards the rear of the column, leaving an order for a regiment of our brigade to follow him at once. My command was detailed for this duty, and on reaching the rear of our column we were deployed as skirmishers and ordered to advance through the woods towards the Chickahominy River. Personally I was completely demoralized by the sudden fright of the explosion and almost ready to run from my own shadow. Pride alone kept me in my place as with beating heart I advanced cautiously through the woods every moment expecting to hear the whistle of a hostile bullet. For half a mile or more, however, nothing disturbed the quietude of our advance save the sound of distant explosions following each other in rapid succession.

Suddenly, off towards my right, I seemed to hear the cries of children. Startled anew by a sound so unexpected in the midst of the forest, with a vivid recollection of the deceptive cries uttered by the Indians in their wars and described so accurately by Cooper,[56] I advanced still more cautiously toward a point where the increased light seemed to indicate a clearing, and from which the cries apparently proceeded. In a few moments the clearing burst into view. In fact I had reached the termination of the forest, and before me lay a succession of green fields sloping gently down to the river, here about half a mile distant. To my right stood a substantial modern man-

47

sion, surrounded, like most southern houses, by a wide verandah, upon which appeared a lady with a babe in her arms and two older children clinging closely to her skirts and sobbing bitterly. A more striking picture of one of the horrors of war has never been presented to my eyes. Advancing to the group I inquired what was the matter. The mother replied that the explosion which so startled my slumbers had shattered every pane of glass in the house, and had frightened them all nearly out of their senses. She had rushed out upon the verandah, fearing that the house was about to fall down, and had then stopped, conscious that she had no place to which she could fly for protection. Comforting the group as well as I could, I looked down towards the river where the sound of explosions still continued and beheld a column of dark smoke rising from the ruins of a bridge over the Chickahominy, while bright flashes of fire and the rattle of exploding shells told the story of the destruction of the enemy's ammunition train. Gen. McClellan, unable to carry off his reserve ammunition on his retreat, had placed it in cars, applied a slow match and started the train for the bridge, where its explosion had overwhelmed everything in one common destruction. The force of the explosion may be judged from the fact that the house whose windows were all shattered was situated at least three-quarters of a mile from the bridge over the river. The explosion thus explained, we retraced our steps to the main column and on the following day crossed the Chickahominy at the so-called "Grapevine Bridge."

It was in this march that the discovery of a ragged hole through the crown of my hat first called my attention to the narrow escape I had made at the battle of Cold Harbor. As an Irish comrade remarked "If ye had been two inches taller ye'd ha been a dead man shure!" The next three days have left little impression upon my recollection save an apparently aimless and interminable wandering through the forests and swamps of the Chickahominy.

MALVERN HILL

About 4 P.M. on Tuesday, July 1st, however, the rattle of musketry and boom of cannon in close proximity to our line of march informed us that we had at last overtaken our retreating foe. Filing into an open field in our front, we had for a few moments a good view of the heights of Malvern Hill—a view too which earned for us a few shots well-aimed, though fortunately at such a distance as to prove ineffective. Yet one shell struck

48

the ground just under the horse of Gen. Jackson, who with his staff had ridden into the field to reconnoiter, but fortunately the missile failed to explode. Here too for the first time I saw a shell in its course from the mouth of the cannon until its explosion. Coming directly towards me, it appeared as a small black object apparently changing its position very little from moment to moment, but gradually enlarging as it approached, until it burst perhaps a hundred yards in my front. Withdrawing speedily from this field where the enemy would soon have found our range, we formed line of battle in the adjacent woods and advanced down a wooded slope to a swampy bottom, where we were ordered to lie down while the shells and cannon-balls whistled furiously through the tree-tops, doing us, however, no harm.

It was now nearly sun-down and, as no order to move reached us, worn out and hungry, I fell fast asleep. I do not know at what hour I awoke, but the rain was falling upon my face and Egyptian darkness surrounded me. For a moment I failed to recall where I was. Then, reaching out on either side I touched my adjacent comrades, arousing them too from sleep. In whispers we exchanged ideas as to where we were and after a few moments I rose from the ground and groped my way to the point where I supposed Capt. Cummings to be. To my surprise I not only failed to find him, but after proceeding a few steps to my right all trace of my regiment was lost. Only some ten or a dozen of us were left together, all on the extreme left of the line. Puzzled at the state of affairs and anxious we held a sort of council of war in the rain and darkness. I remembered having seen a line of battle in front of us when I lay down and volunteered to go forward and see if it was still there. Groping my way cautiously to the front, I stumbled over the prostrate form of a man, and asking in a low tone what regiment he belonged to, received the non-committal answer "What regiment do you belong to?" Replying that I was a member of the 9th Louisiana regiment, he said he belonged to the —th Virginia. I then inquired if he knew what had become of the regiment in his rear. He said he did not, but had heard the noise of some troops moving there some little time before. Returning to my companions we discussed anxiously our position and our most judicious course of action, and finally decided, in the absolute uncertainty of all our surroundings, to remain quietly where we were until daylight should at least enable us to see what we were doing. Accordingly we again lay down and listened with anxious ears to the distant rumbling of artillery which alone disturbed the silence of the night. Finally however, we all once more fell asleep and rested quietly until aroused by the advent of daylight.

49

The rain was still falling dismally as, wet cold and hungry, we endeavored to retrace our steps of the preceding day. As we ascended the slope down which we had advanced I noticed the results of a cannon-ball which gave me a better idea of the force of these missiles than I had ever had before. A small knotty and gnarly white oak tree, about sixteen inches in diameter at its base, had been pierced squarely by a solid shot, which had killed a man lying behind the tree, while, such was the toughness and tenacity of the wood, the hole made by the ball was entirely closed by a mass of interlacing splinters, so that it was impossible to see through the opening. As we progressed towards our supposed rear we overtook numerous stragglers, bent, like ourselves, on finding their commands, and about 9 A.M. we ran upon our own regiment bivouacking in the woods and struggling to build fires for a cup of coffee.

On inquiry the explanation of our abandonment of the night before was very simple. About sun-down the regiments upon the right of our brigade received from some unknown officer an order to advance, which they did at the expense of a decided repulse and the loss of many valuable lives. The left of the line failed to receive the order, nor in the darkness of the swampy glade did they notice for some time the advance of the right. As the latter, however, retired from their futile charge, the right companies of my regiment observed their withdrawal, and the command was whispered along the line to follow their steps. We, who occupied the extreme left of the line and were probably sleeping, heard nothing of the movement and were left in our places. We found the whole brigade so scattered and disorganized that a halt for most of the remainder of the day was necessary to collect the stragglers. Indeed the whole battle of Malvern Hill seems to have been conducted on the part of the Confederates without system or mutual co-operation, and with the natural result of a complete defeat. Fortunately the Federal army was equally disorganized and still more dispirited than our own, and retreated after the battle to the protection of the gun-boats on the James River.

Advancing once more on the road to the James River, on July 4th we once again came in sight of the enemy. Here hungry, dirty and thoroughly worn out, the usual elasticity of my spirits failed me, and the order to advance in line of battle across a wide open field against the enemy, supposed to be concealed in the woods at its further border, filled me with the gloomiest presentiments. I felt sure that I should fall in this field, and any reasonable excuse for absenting myself from the charge would have been eagerly

50

seized. But none such came, and too proud to slink away from danger, I gritted my teeth and moved forward with my command to what I fully believed to be my death. Laughably enough not a gun was fired, and we entered the coveted woods as sound as we started. After tarrying for a few days before McClellan's position on the James River, we withdrew to the vicinity of Richmond, where a short breathing-spell was afforded us for rest and refreshment, and, as my thirst for experience upon the battle field was now fully quenched, I resumed my duties in the Quartermaster's Department gladly, and with the determination never again to seek danger when my duty did not plainly demand it of me.

IN THE QUARTERMASTER'S DEPARTMENT

Our respite, however was of short duration,[57] and on the 17th of July we once more took up our march and proceeded to Gordonsville.[58] A short delay here was followed by an advance across the Rapidan River and the bloody battle of Cedar Mountain, fought on Saturday, August 9th, 1862, about eight miles south of Culpeper. In this battle I took no part, remaining at my post in the Q. M. Department and witnessing no more of the contest than an incipient stampede of our wagon trains due to some absurd rumor and for a few moments threatening serious results.

On the 11th we returned to Gordonsville, but on the arrival of reinforcements from Richmond we once more crossed the Rapidan and begun the wonderful flank march which resulted in the second battle of Bull Run and the complete discomfiture of Pope.[59] The invasion of Maryland, the capture of Harper's Ferry and the drawn battle of Sharpsburg or Antietam followed, but during the whole of this glorious and bloody period I continued at my post with the wagon train, which most of the time lay encamped near Ashby's Gap, advancing by September 16th to Winchester. Nothing important disturbed our quiet during this period save a threatened attack from the enemy's cavalry, which we fortunately succeeded in "bluffing off" by the display of a few old muskets and a piece of artillery which had, for some reason, been left in our charge.[60]

In the hard-fought battle of Sharpsburg, Archie Gordon, a noble and handsome young fellow, second lieutenant of my company, met his death,[61] and as soon as the exigencies of active service permitted an election, the company chose me to fill his place, although I was not present with them

51

and had not shared in the terrible trials and struggles of the last bloody month. As soon as I heard of the unexpected honor bestowed upon me by my comrades I rejoined my command, then near Martinsburg, and entered at once upon the active duties of a line officer. For the next two months, however, these consisted in little more than tearing up the track of the Baltimore and Ohio R. R. and an occasional tour of picket or scouting duty, labors which did not prevent our thorough enjoyment of the beauties of a glorious autumn in the Shenandoah Valley.

About Nov. 1st,[62] in the absence of the regimental quartermaster, Capt. Hughes, I was again detailed to take his position, though only for a short period, and by the middle of the month we had left the Valley and proceeded, via Orange C. H., to the familiar banks of the Rappahannock. For the next month our duty consisted principally in picketing the river below Fredericksburg, for which purpose we even descended the stream as far as Port Royal, some 25 miles below.

BATTLE OF FREDERICKSBURG

Our sojourn in this neighborhood was enlivened by the acquaintance of a number of Virginia families, with whom a few of our officers became quite intimate, and the dull routine of military life by day was relieved by parties and visits at night, which on some occasions scarcely terminated before daylight.

This fortune was, however, too good to last, and on the 12th of December, 1862, we suddenly received orders to march at once to Hamilton's Crossing,[63] a station on the Richmond and Fredericksburg R. R., about five miles south of Fredericksburg. The night was starlight, but bitterly cold, and at each halt in the march the men started fires to warm their chilled members and fell asleep standing or sitting as circumstances permitted. A longer and more wearisome night I have never experienced, but as the sun rose cloudless in the morning and the roar of artillery close at hand indicated the approach of battle, we all brightened up in anticipation of the approaching conflict. As we marched towards the field of battle a solid shot, whose force was chiefly spent, struck the road about thirty yards in advance of my regiment and, ricochetting gracefully five or ten feet over our heads, passed on to the rear without damage, resembling greatly the bound of an ordinary ball, and almost tempting one to try to catch it. We took position at first in a sunken road just at Hamilton's Crossing in rear of the main line of battle, which occupied a wooded crest in our front. About eleven o'clock, however, we were ordered forward at the "double-quick," and, as we plunged into the woods in our front, where the shells were bursting with rapidity and considerable accuracy, I caught my foot in a twisted vine and fell as if shot. Indeed, both my comrades and I myself for a moment believed that I had been hit: but rising hastily and shaking myself to make sure of the presence of all my limbs, I hurried forward to my position in line and advanced with my command to the crest of the hills, where one of our batteries was carrying on a fierce duel with those of the enemy in the plain below. Just at this moment Jackson and a portion of his staff galloped madly to the crest where our battery was posted, and I shall never forget the incarnation of war presented by his face at this moment. Coolly he sat upon his horse in the midst of the infernal roar of cannon and bursting shells, whose fragments swept the exposed crest like a tornado, and calmly but sharply scanned the field before him. Meanwhile, we, having reached the same crest of the hills, were ordered to lie down, and I remember well how closely I hugged the earth, while shell and shot tore the air above me with a sound like the hasty ripping of stout canvas, only intensely magnified. After a few moments, which, however, seemed to us an age, we were ordered back a few rods beneath the crest of the hill for protection and to support the battery of which mention has been made, and remained in this position the remainder of the day. An occasional shot or shell passing over our heads informed us that the enemy was still in our front, but no further active struggle occurred in our vicinity.

The night was again cold and clear, and as we huddled together in line of battle to make the most of our scanty blankets, even fatigue scarcely sufficed to bring any continuous sleep to my eyes. At last, chilled to the marrow, and weary of turning from side to side in the vain effort to extract a little warmth from my companions, I rose from the ground and paced up and down the line of battle in the hope of stimulating the sluggish blood-currents by a little exercise. It must have been one or two o'clock in the morning, and the bright moonlight varnished with a silvery sheen the bare twigs and withered leaves of the forest, defining them almost as distinctly as the day. Apparently I was the only soul awake, and as I looked down the long white line of battle, where the men lay wrapped in their blankets, it seemed more like a row of corpses wrapped in their winding-sheets than a line of living and breathing warriors. Scarcely a sound disturbed the intense silence. Even the owls and other birds of the night seemed to respect the slumbers of my exhausted comrades. Our bivouac was situated at the head of a broad and rather shallow ravine or valley, filled with undergrowth and small trees and debouching into the broad plain which bordered the Rappahannock. As I looked across the tops of the brush and trees a dense veil of misty clouds shut out the valley beyond, but occasionally the solemn stillness of the night was broken by a faint and ghostly wail, which located itself at no special point, but seemed to rise like a mist from the face of the whole field of battle and conveyed the impression of wide spread and terrible anguish.

The unutterable sadness of that midnight wail from the battlefield of Fredericksburg has never left, and will never leave, my mind and memory. After a time, wearied and somewhat warmed by my exercise, I again lay down and fell into a deep sleep, from which I was awakened by the stir of the opening day. The next two days were passed in expectation of a renewal of the assault upon our lines, which thus far had seemed rather a feint than a serious attack. The terrible slaughter of the enemy in front of Marye's Hill on our left was but imperfectly known to us, and we had no idea that the battle was now over. Their retreat across the river was, therefore, very much of a surprise, as we had not anticipated so easy and speedy a victory.

It is now well known that Gen. Burnside,[64] the commander of the Federal army, had intended to renew the attack upon our position, but was deterred by the advice and pleadings of his subordinate officers and the manifest demoralization of his troops. It is also related that a council of war was held by Gen. Lee on the night preceding the withdrawal of the Federals, to consider the advisability of attacking them in their then position. Gen. Jackson, who of course attended the council, was so fatigued by his exertions of the preceding days that he fell asleep during the deliberations, and when partially awakened to express his opinion is said to have merely said "Drive them into the river! Drive them into the river!" and then to have relapsed once more into slumber. It is difficult to say what would have been the effect of a determined attack upon the Federals after the failure of their first assault. The plain which they occupied was completely commanded by their artillery on the Stafford heights, and these guns would doubtless have inflicted severe loss upon us before we could have got to close quarters, but once among them they would have been masked by the danger of killing their own men. At all events Gen. Lee did not see fit to make the attempt, and the Federals effected a safe retreat without other loss than the terrible slaughter of the actual battle. The remainder of the winter was spent along the Rappahannock, either in winter-quarters or on tours of picket duty, though, for

54

a time, in consequence of the illness of Capt. Hughes, the regimental quartermaster, I was again detailed in charge of his department.[65]

CHANCELLORSVILLE CAMPAIGN

As evidences of the coming spring multiplied in the woods and fields, renewed activity in inspections, reviews, drills etc. warned us that the season of active operations was once more at hand. On Wednesday, April 29th, 1863, the reappearance of the Federals on the southern bank of the Rappahannock below Fredericksburg informed us that the campaign had opened. For a day or two active skirmishing alone took place in our front, and it was soon discovered that the main point of attack was higher up the river, where Gen. Hooker[66] with the major portion of his force had crossed and was already involved in the intricacies of the Wilderness. Accordingly on Thursday night the greater part of the Confederate army faced to the rear and hastened to meet the foe in his chosen position. Early's division,[67] of which my brigade formed a part, and Barksdale's brigade of McLaws's division,[68] were left to hold in check the enemy before Fredericksburg. Early on Sunday morning, May 3d, my brigade was ordered to "double-quick" from Hamilton's Crossing on the extreme right of the Confederate line to Taylor's Hill, above Fredericksburg and on the extreme left of the line, a distance of about five miles. Our route followed closely the Confederate line of battle, just in rear of which our course was taken, and of course at many points we were exposed to a sharp fire from the enemy's artillery and skirmishers. Our loss, however, was slight (apparently more from good luck than good management), and, after a fatiguing race, a small portion of the brigade, breathless, drenched with perspiration and utterly fagged-out, reached our destination and gladly seized the opportunity of resting in the rifle-pits and trenches already constructed. I doubt whether more than two hundred men composed the advance of our force. The remainder were dragging along, as best they might, over the rough and dangerous road we were compelled to follow. Gradually, however, these stragglers came up, until a respectable force was finally gathered around us. But our arrival was none too soon, for, just at the foot of the hill, Gibbon's Federal division[69] was preparing to seize our position. Fortunately a small canal, which here crossed our front in the valley below, had delayed the enemy and thus afforded us time to gain the defenses of the hill. Our appearance upon the scene apparently discouraged the advance of the Federals, who soon withdrew from our immediate front, and the occasional bullet of a sharpshooter was all that disturbed our contemplation of a scene of beauty and interest, such as has never since fallen to my lot to behold. The morning was bright and beautiful, and from our lofty position on Taylor's Hill the lovely valley of the Rappahannock was visible far down the river to our right. In our front the division of Gibbon, foiled in its purpose of seizing the hill, retired slowly, coolly and in excellent order, in spite of considerable annoyance from one of our batteries. Further to the right the batteries of the enemy in hot service were plainly visible, and the occasional explosion of a caisson or smashing of a gun-carriage told of the excellent practice of the Confederate guns opposed to them. Finally, still further to the right, the alternate charge and retreat of several lines of battle were plainly visible, while the opposing shouts and cheers of the combatants, as they were borne to our ears, revealed the changing results of the battle. The whole scene lay like a panorama before us, and it required an occasional shot from the enemy in our front to divest us of the idea that the whole affair was a beautiful and life-like picture, or a sham battle exhibited for our amusement.

In a short time, however, greatly to our surprise, we received orders to retreat as quickly as possible from our almost impregnable position, and soon learned that the enemy had finally succeeded in carrying Marye's Hill on our right, and were likely to cut us off from the remainder of the army. A hurried march of two or three hours brought us to a position of comparative security on Telegraph Road and restored our communications with the remainder of our division, and, forming here in line of battle, we bivouacked for the night in a wood of considerable extent, where we remained undisturbed by the enemy. The most of the following day was consumed in maneuvering and awaiting further aid from Gen. Lee to enable us to resume the offensive. Finally about 5 P.M. my brigade was conducted by a circuitous route through a deep ravine[70] to the foot of an enormous hill, which I now believe to have been the same Taylor's Hill from which we had retreated the day before. Here we were drawn up in line of battle and ordered to await the signal of three guns upon our left. The men spent the interval in snatching a hasty supper (for many of them their last) of crackers and bacon, chatting, smoking and jesting as if danger were the last thing in their minds.

Before us rose the hill to a height which shut out any prospect of the summit, while its sides were covered with brush and fallen timber to such a degree than an orderly ascent was utterly impossible. An occasional head was seen peering down upon us from the crest, and was presumably that of an enemy, but not a shot disturbed the security of the quiet valley in which we stood watching the lengthening shadows cast by the declining sun. At last the signal guns boomed forth upon the quiet air, and with a shout of "Charge" Gen. Harry Hays launched us up the hill on a full run.[71] Of course military order was out of the question. Each man made a route for himself and rushed for the summit. My long legs and good wind enabled me to keep a place among the foremost, and when our advance reached the crest of the hill we halted for a moment to await the approach of our less speedy comrades. But our appearance was the signal for a cross-fire of artillery and musketry which seemed to make the very air boil. Men fell on every side, and, without further delay and with another shout of "Charge," Gen. Hays again led us forward against an enemy as yet unseen but manifestly not far off.

On we rushed across an open plateau, along the further border of which a high brush fence opposed a formidable obstacle to our advance. As I approached the fence, which in front of me was fully breast-high, I hesitated for a moment what course to pursue; whether to tear open a passage through it, or to try to jump it. Short time, however, was afforded for reflection, and, as a shell shrieked by my ear, I rose with a tremendous leap and, as I cleared the brush, saw before me with dismay a sunken road[72] about eight or ten feet deep, into which I fell in a heap upon the heads and backs of a number of Federals, who from this natural defense had been furnishing us with a hot reception. It is hard to say which of us was most surprised, and for a moment I thought my time had come. But numbers of my comrades, after a somewhat similar experience, poured into the cut, and the enemy at once surrendered. Leaving them to take care of themselves, however, we clambered out of the other side of the roadway and rushed forward once more to complete our victory. By this time, of course, all semblance of military order had been totally lost. Captains lost their companies, and companies and regiments were so intermingled that the brigade formed simply a howling, rushing and firing mob, without pretense of organization or authority. Somewhat blown by my exertions, and badly shaken by my unexpected jump into the roadway, I gradually drifted behind the mass of my comrades, and in spite of my utmost exertions, soon found myself almost alone, save a few stragglers, who, like myself, had been unable to keep up the headlong rush of the advance.

Considerably to my left and upon the slope of a gentle elevation I observed a Federal brigade drawn up in line of battle, and in their front an officer mounted upon a magnificent white horse, who seemed vainly to urge his men to advance. Waving his sword above his head he rode forward a few paces, while not a man in the ranks seemed willing to follow his example. At last, as if ashamed not to follow their brave leader, the line rushed forward some hundred yards to a line of rifle-pits in their front and began a sharp fire of musketry upon the Confederate force advancing against them. This forward movement of the enemy placed them on a line with me, or even somewhat in my rear, although in my immediate front no considerable firing was then taking place. Accordingly, I continued to advance through a slight wood which covered the slope of the hill, and soon came up again with our own force, which had just occupied the reverse side of a line of rifle-pits which ran along the crest of the ridge. At this moment a violent fire of musketry was opened upon them from the Federal reserves, and it was only with considerable risk that I was able to gain the shelter of the embankment of earth thrown up in front of the pits. This embankment was not more than fifteen to twenty inches high, and the whistle of Minié balls and scattering of earth from the top of the slight defense behind which we lay warned everyone to hug the ground closely if he wished to escape injury. Beside me, as I lay on the ground, I found the Lieut. Col. of my regiment, but most of the men in my neighborhood were total strangers, belonging to other regiments of the brigade. Once I raised my head cautiously above the embankment and took a hasty survey of our immediate front. A dense smoke obscured vision, but I caught a glimpse through the murky air of a line of the enemy, apparently oblique to our line of battle and to its right, standing and firing rapidly. As I withdrew my head I shouted to the Lieut. Col. "Let us charge" and half rose from the ground. He shook his head, however, rather deprecatingly, and I lay down again, filled with regret that at this crisis of the battle no leader appeared to direct and cheer us forward. Our attack had lost its momentum, and, so far as offense was concerned, we were powerless from confusion and lack of organization. In a few moments I observed the extreme right of our line begin to retreat, not at first en masse, but man after man retired slowly down the slope which we had just ascended. As the movement extended to the left it became more rapid and simultaneous, and finally I caught sight of our Adjutant rushing down the slope at a pace which made his coat-tails stream out horizontally behind him.

Realizing at once that disaster had befallen us, I rose hastily and tore

58

down the slope to the rear at the top of my speed, the voice of the Lieut. Col. vainly calling to me to return. I had run scarcely more than twenty steps when a dull blow upon my right shoulder knocked me over, while my sword flew from my hand some ten feet away. Rising hastily, I shook myself to see if I was all there, and finding nothing apparently materially wrong, I picked up my sword and continued my retreat, but at a slower pace. Some rods further back I ran across a comrade who had been shot in the ankle and was hobbling from the field, and lending him my arm I assisted him to a rail fence, behind which he was able to protect himself to some extent from the balls which still hissed about us. Observing the brigade endeavoring to rally at a point still further in the rear, I directed my steps thither, conscious now that my right arm was stiff and numb, but supposing it the result of a contusion from a spent ball. On my road I overtook Lieut. Bringhurst of my company, and on my telling him my experience, he informed me that there was a ragged hole in the shoulder of my coat and advised me to seek the field hospital.

After considerable difficulty, occasioned by the darkness and the uncertainty of the location of the hospital, I finally found this institution in an old barn about half a mile in rear of the battlefield, and reporting to Surgeon Love of my regiment, was directed to remove my clothing for examination. The ball had struck me on the back of the large muscles of the neck and shoulder, penetrated the strap of my haversack, and, ranging inward and forward, had lodged in the right side of my neck close upon the carotid artery. Half an inch further would have inevitably ended my military career! Lying down upon the rough operating table, Surg. Love speedily extracted the ball through a small incision, and sewing up the wound, directed me to dress it and the opening in the shoulder with cold water. Worn out with fatigue and excitement, I lay down upon a convenient blanket and was soon lost to temporal troubles.

The morning broke bright and beautiful, but as I rose from my blanket I was shocked to see the number of my comrades lying around me suffering from wounds of every description. I learned on inquiry that Capt. Cummings had been killed upon the field with a number of his company, that Col. Stafford and the Lieut. Col. Williams were missing, and that our attack, though finally repulsed, had resulted in the retreat of the enemy across Banks's Ford.

In a day or two those of us who were able to be removed were placed upon the cars and sent to Richmond, where we were distributed among the various hospitals of that city.[73] I was assigned to "Hospital No. 10," or the "Officers' Hospital," a large brick building on Main Street, conducted as a pay hospital, chiefly for officers. Here I was fortunate enough to secure a room with the comrade whom I had assisted from the battlefield a few days before, and I found the house surgeon also an old acquaintance from Rapides. My wound healed rapidly, and in the course of ten days was almost entirely closed. It was our custom on retiring for the night to turn our gas down low, but not to entirely extinguish it. My comrade and I had retired as usual, and, rested and refreshed by quiet and good food, I was feeling almost absolutely well. I slept soundly until after midnight, when I was aroused by a vivid dream, which awoke me with a sudden start. I thought, or rather dreamed, that my wound had broken out afresh, and, as I awoke, I involuntarily thrust my hand to my neck. With horror and affright I felt the blood spurting forth in a stream, and found the bed quite soaked with the crimson fluid. Hastily calling to my comrade, who at once turned up the gas, I discovered a small stream, about the size of a knitting-needle, spurting out for a foot from my wound, and the house surgeon, who was immediately summoned, found some little difficulty in checking the hemorrhage from a small artery which had opened in the line of the incision made for the extraction of the ball. However, by the simple application of ice he finally succeeded, and the wound thereafter never gave any serious trouble. It was six weeks, however, before I was considered fit to return to my command, although the last fortnight of my sojourn in Richmond, between picnics, parties etc., was a genuine holiday.

IN SEARCH OF THE ARMY

About June 20th, 1863, I started to rejoin my command, travelling via Gordonsville to Staunton, where I was delayed several days in order to join a company of some hundred convalescents, who were to be forwarded to their several regiments. In association with several other officers en route for their commands I was placed in charge of this squad of convalescents, and we started from Staunton by way of the valley turnpike, for Winchester, where we were to report for further orders. Such a heterogenous battalion as was placed under our orders could of course be controlled only very imperfectly, and in two or three days the stragglers far outnumbered those who kept up with the command, and by the time we

60

reached Winchester not more than a dozen of us comprised all the squad of convalescents ready to report for duty. Here we secured rations and took a short rest.

No reliable information as to the exact position of the Army of Northern Virginia was attainable. It was said to be somewhere in Maryland or Pennsylvania, but whether we should be able to rejoin it seemed quite problematical. Nevertheless some fifty or more of us, most of whom were officers, decided to make the attempt. Accordingly we once more started forward, repeating our experience of losses by straggling, until on arriving at Martinsburg probably not more than twenty of us remained together. Here the air was filled with rumors of all kinds. Lee was in Maryland, in Pennsylvania, before Washington, defeated and retreating, had secured a great victory, etc. Nothing certain was known of the whereabouts and condition of the army, and, after some hesitation, about a dozen of us decided to go forwards at all hazards until we could gain some definite information to guide us further.

Leaving Martinsburg, we took the road to Williamsport, but after proceeding a few miles were met by the report that Williamsport was occupied by the Federal cavalry. Though this rumor could not be definitely authenticated, it discouraged a number of our party, who decided to return, while the remainder of us pushed on to see for ourselves the real condition of affairs. On arriving at Williamsport we found the report untrue and, crossing the Potomac into Maryland, pushed forward again for Hagerstown, Greencastle and Chambersburg, living on the scanty contents of our haversacks and such food as we could buy or beg from the inhabitants. Although we followed the direct track of the Confederate army, I observed comparatively few marks of the devastation commonly marking the route of an invading host, though of course provisions of all kinds were very scarce and in some places the crops had been trampled down by the feet of the soldiers. The inhabitants seemed rather dazed by the unexpected change in the face of the war, and while by no means cordial in their reception of our little party, took no active part in annoying us or in hindering our advance. On one occasion, observing an old Dutch farmer sitting on his porch as we were passing his house, I stopped to ask a light for my pipe, presenting my request in as polite a manner as was possible. The old farmer, however, did not wait to hear the close of my sentence, but replied hastily "No. Soldiers got it all!" With a laugh I passed on, leaving the old man to his morose meditations.

61

On arriving at Chambersburg we found the city occupied by Pickett's division[74] of Lee's army, and found considerable difficulty in procuring rations from the commissary, who declined to furnish supplies to unorganized bodies of troops. Finally two or three of us made our way to Gen. Pickett's headquarters and presented our claims, when the general swore a round oath that we should have rations if the commissary had to seize all the cattle in the country. Of course we had no further difficulty. On the afternoon of July 1st we again started for Gettysburg, where our army was understood to be concentrating, and, after a march of five or six miles, bivouacked by the roadside in a little belt of woodland. At some time during the night I was awakened by the tramp of horses, and, opening my eyes, saw Gen. Pickett and his staff ride by, and the steady tramp of his division marching to the front informed me that active service was probably close at hand.

The next morning our squad of convalescents proceeded through Fayetteville, Greenwood and Cashtown towards Gettysburg, arriving near Willoughby Run about sundown. The thunder of artillery had sounded in our ears all day, and at this point evidences of a sharp struggle met our eyes. From an occasional straggler or teamster we learned some details of the battle, and several officers and men of our party learned the positions of their commands and pushed on at once to rejoin them. I could, however, obtain no satisfactory information of the whereabouts of the Louisiana troops, and decided, rather than waste my time and strength in following unknown roads in the darkness, to await the light of morning before seeking further my command.

Snatching a hasty breakfast, by sunrise the next morning I started alone across the battlefield of July 1st. The ground was covered with the débris of clothing, cartridges, knapsacks, etc., and furrowed by the wheels of artillery, while here and there a Federal soldier, still unburied, lay festering on the trampled and torn grass. As I hurried across this field of blood, casting now and then a shy glance at the horrors which surrounded me, I was shocked to see at a considerable distance to my right a wounded Federal rise to a sitting posture and gaze wildly at me as I hastened forward. Without either food or water to relieve his sufferings, I felt that I could do nothing for him, and yet I have ever since regretted that I did not at least receive his last words and extend to him the sympathy of a fellow-soldier, whose fate in a few hours might be entirely similar. But I was nervously anxious to rejoin my companions, and alone on this field of slaughter I felt timid and unnerved. Accordingly, I only added speed to my steps and soon left the battlefield and its horrors behind.

About 9 A.M. I learned from a teamster that the Louisiana troops were occupying the town of Gettysburg, from which, in ignorance of the roads, I had wandered away considerably to the north and west. Changing my course to the point indicated, I was happy about 11 o'clock to find my regiment resting upon the pavement of one of the streets of the town, while the men were mostly eating, smoking or snatching a hasty nap. After the first hearty salutations were over, I learned that the brigade on the preceding evening had stormed Cemetery Hill,[75] captured a battery there posted and then been driven out by fresh forces of the enemy who assailed them in the darkness. The engagement had been severe, and had cost the lives of a considerable number of my brigade, among them the adjutant of my regiment.[76] My own company at this time was skirmishing in the outskirts of the town, and one of the men who happened to be present volunteered to guide me to my comrades. Accordingly we proceeded towards the southern edge of the town, and scurrying hastily across the main street, which was swept by the bullets of the enemy's skirmishers, made our way through gardens and enclosures to a large, frame house, into the back door of which we entered.

Here an amusing sight met my view. Around a table in the center of the room were gathered the majority of my company, engaged in discussing a generous meal, apparently procured by ransacking the pantry and cellar of the mansion, while at each of the front windows a couple of men were occasionally exchanging shots with the enemy, being relieved at intervals by their comrades and retiring to join in the feast until their turn once more came around. Of course I met with a hearty welcome, and learning that an outpost was placed at the foot of the garden, I asked one of the men to lead me to the spot. Passing through a gate leading to the garden, we scampered at full speed across an open space of about one hundred yards to the shelter of another house, still nearer the enemy, behind which I found half-a-dozen comrades skirmishing with a force of the enemy a short distance below. One man had taken position behind a large oak tree, standing some ten or fifteen feet from the corner of the house, and from this coign of vantage was steadily firing upon his antagonists. The latter had discovered the range very accurately, and the torn bark of the tree bore witness to the precision of their

63

aim, while the whistle of bullets through the interval between the house and the tree warned us to keep well under cover. After watching the duel for a few moments, a sudden exclamation from the man behind the tree attracted my attention, and on looking at him I saw that he had been shot through the right arm, which had been incautiously exposed. It was now something of a problem how to get him under the protection of the corner of the house behind which we were sheltered. Finally I directed him to lie down flat upon the ground, extending his legs towards the house, and, awaiting a temporary lull in the firing, two of us rushed out suddenly, seized him hastily by the feet and dragged him across the dangerous interval and behind the shelter, where we dressed his wound temporarily and laid him in the shade, not daring to carry him through the exposed garden before night.

About 1 P.M. a tremendous outburst of artillery announced that some new movement was in progress. Never before or since have I listened to such an uproar, which fairly made the earth tremble and the air vibrate with successive shocks, as nearly 150 cannon opened upon the position of the enemy. Of course we did not know at the time just what this uproar indicated, and it was not until evening that we heard of the now famous charge and repulse of Pickett's division, which concluded the bloody battle of Gettysburg.

As night drew her mantle of darkness over the town our skirmishers were drawn in and rejoined their regiments, and before daylight we withdrew slowly and sullenly to the ridge in rear of the town, where we proceeded to strengthen our position with earthworks and to prepare for our retreat. Here we spent the Fourth of July listening to the music of the bands of the Federal host and awaiting the anticipated attack. During the night of the same day we began to withdraw, but it was not until 9 A. M. of the 5th that my brigade took up its march along the Fairfield road towards the Potomac and Virginia.

RETREAT TO VIRGINIA

Of the occurrences of the next ten days my memory preserves only the dim picture of tedious and rainy marches by night, and wearying, anxious haltings in line of battle by day, until early on the morning of July 14th we crossed a pontoon bridge at Falling Waters and gladly set foot once more on what seemed the homelike soil of "Old Virginny." The weariness

64

of this retreat was greatly alleviated, so far as I was concerned, by my promotion to the position of Adjutant of my regiment on July 4th, a post which entitled me to the luxury of a horse. Indeed I succeeded at once to the horse and boots of the late Adjutant, Lieut. R. T. Crawford, who, as already said, was killed in the assault upon Cemetery Hill the night before my arrival in Gettysburg. I mention particularly the boots, because at this period they formed an item of no inconsiderable importance in the uniform of a Confederate officer, and constituted a rare outfit for an officer of inferior rank.

With very little delay we now marched up the Shenandoah Valley, via Winchester, Strasburg, and Newmarket to Luray, and thence through Fisher's Gap to Madison Court House and the vicinity of Gordonsville, where we arrived about August 1st. Here a long rest of about two months was afforded our weary men, and in the scanty pleasures of camp life we partially forgot the trials of the past and prepared ourselves for those of the future.

ASSISTANT ADJUTANT GENERAL

On the eighth of October 1863, Col. Stafford was appointed a Brigadier General in the Confederate service, and, considerably to my surprise, selected me as his Assistant Adjutant General. I say "to my surprise," because, while well equipped in a literary sense for the duties of this position, I had little or no experience in the command of men and the details of duty in so important a staff position. I did not feel willing, however, to decline the preferred honor, and braced myself for an earnest effort to discharge the duties of the enlarged field thus opened to me. Just at this period Gen. Lee began his flank march around Meade, which terminated in the retreat of the latter to Centerville and the sharp and bloody engagement of Oct. 14th at Bristoe Station. Gen. Stafford was assigned to a brigade of Louisiana troops, consisting of the 1st, 2nd, 10th, 14th and 15th Louisiana regiments, and forming a part of the division of Maj. Gen. Edward Johnson.[77] Accordingly, he and I bade farewell to our old comrades and set forth on horseback to find our new command. As the whole army was on the move, this search occupied several days, and when we overtook the brigade we found them on the march, with little opportunity for making the acquaintance of their new commander. Indeed, in the want of all ordinary facilities for writing, I was compelled to draw up with a pencil and upon a stray slip of paper found in my pocket-book the order announcing Gen.

65

Stafford's assumption of the command, and in the absence of couriers to present it to the regimental commanders myself.

Our reception was by no means warm, nor do I think the regimental officers of the brigade ever regarded us otherwise than in the light of interlopers, who had deprived them of well-earned promotion. Col. Williams of the 2d Louisiana regiment, the senior colonel commanding the brigade, was a good-natured and gentlemanly planter, loved for his manly qualities, but by no means an ideal officer. Though not lacking in ambition, he never displayed any resentment at what undoubtedly seemed to him an unjust over-slaugh of his reasonable claims. Upon the staff of the brigade when Gen. Stafford assumed command were Capt. Alexander Boarman,[78] Inspector, Lieut. D. T. Merrick,[79] aide-de-camp and Maj. Francis Rawle as Quartermaster. Boarman was an able and ambitious young lawyer of Shreveport who had anticipated for himself the position of chief of the brigade staff, and never really forgave what he considered my usurpation of his claims. Capable and well acquainted with the composition of the brigade and the duties of a staff officer, he might have been of the utmost service in initiating me into the details of my new duties, had he been so disposed, and might have saved me some mortifying mistakes into which my inexperience led me. But he simply looked on with a cold and cynical smile, manifestly enjoying my hesitation and blunders. We always, however, maintained the external forms of politeness, and never exchanged a harsh word while we were associated together both on duty and in prison. Lieut. Merrick was a hair-brained youth, brave to a fault and caring for little save the fun of life.[80] A pleasant and jovial companion, the duties of an aide exactly suited his aspirations and his capacity. Maj. Rawle was a sterling officer and a genial and pleasant gentleman, entirely devoted to the multitudinous and exacting duties of his department.

The battle of Bristoe Station, which brought little credit to the Confederate arms, was fought on Wednesday, October 14th, by the corps of A. P. Hill, and Ewell's corps, to which our brigade belonged, only arrived on the battlefield a short time before sun-down, too late to take any active part in the engagement. As the Federal army during the night made good its retreat to Centerville, the next few days were consumed in the destruction of the Orange and Alexandria R. R., after which we in turn retired slowly behind the Rappahannock and prepared to erect our winter quarters. In this, how-ever, we counted without our host; for on November 7th Meade forced a crossing of the Rappahannock, capturing a considerable portion of Hays's

66

Louisiana brigade (my old command) at Rappahannock Station, and on the following night Lee withdrew behind the Rapidan river.

BATTLE OF PAYNE'S FARM

Here we went into winter quarters in earnest, the cantonment of my brigade being located on Mountain Run, not far from Morton's Ford of the Rapidan. But again our quiet was disturbed by the restless Meade, who on November 27th crossed his army at several of the lower fords of the Rapidan, and, wheeling sharply to the right, endeavored to take our line of defense in flank. As our division occupied the extreme right of Gen. Lee's line, we were at once ordered to face the enemy and endeavor to discover his force and his intentions. Accordingly, crossing Mine Run and advancing through a heavily timbered region, we were greatly surprised while marching quietly along the road to hear firing in our rear, and to learn that our ambulances had been fired upon by the enemy, who was supposed to be in our front and at some little distance. Line of battle was at once formed, though the precise position of the enemy was quite uncertain, and advancing through a stretch of woods we came into an open field, where a hot fire was opened upon us from the enemy's line, which seemed to be formed almost at right angles to our own line and upon our left flank. Hastily changing front to the left we ascended a slight hill, from the summit of which the enemy was seen occupying a piece of woods and pouring into us from its shelter a sharp fire of musketry. Several efforts were made to charge the hostile line, but as these attempts were made by single brigades, without proper deliberation and without co-operation on the part of the other forces to the right and left, they naturally resulted in nothing but the loss of a considerable number of lives. No general officer seemed to direct the movements of the entire body of troops, and we finally settled down to hold the crest of our hill, exchanging a sharp musketry fire with our adversaries, who fortunately were about as bewildered as ourselves at the unexpected conflict.

It seems that French's corps of Meade's army, having crossed the Rapidan at Jacob's Ford en route for Robertson's Tavern, had lost its way and, taking a road too far to the right, had struck the flank of our line advancing from Bartley's Mill to the same point. Soon after dark it was discovered accidentally that the brigade upon our left had been withdrawn to the road. Accord-

67

ingly, in the absence of any orders from the division commander to guide us, Gen. Stafford, fearing that we should be cut off from the remainder of the division in the darkness, gave the order to withdraw to the road from which we had advanced. Here we bivouacked for the night, and in the morning, finding an entire corps of the enemy in our front, we retired again across Mine Run to the protection of the defenses erected along that stream.[81]

The next four days were spent in awaiting and preparing for the threatened attack of Meade; but on Tuesday morning, Nov. 31st, [sic] it was found that the latter, discouraged at the task before him, had abandoned his undertaking and withdrawn quietly to the other side of the Rapidan river. Accordingly we too returned to our quarters on Mountain Run and settled down once more to the monotonous duties of camp life. In my own case, however, this monotony was diversified, if not enlivened, by a number of little unpleasantnesses, due partly to my own inexperience and partly to the peculiarities of my position. For a month or two after my promotion to the position of chief of staff to Gen. Stafford, my commission of Captain did not reach me, and, accordingly, I occupied the anomalous situation of a second lieutenant in actual rank wielding the authority of a captain on the staff. This anomaly exposed me to invidious remarks and by no means favored proper military subordination. Regimental adjutants, who bore the rank of first lieutenants, chafed at receiving orders from an inferior in rank, and especially from one regarded as a virtual interloper. This proceeded so far that on one occasion I anticipated a duel might be the result. Coolness and firm, but conciliatory conduct, averted the danger. Gen. Stafford himself took little or no interest in the ordinary routine of official duty and almost invariably referred all petitions, reports, etc., requiring his consideration and signature, to me, authorizing me even to sign his name. Indeed in this latter duty I became such an expert, that I greatly doubt whether the General himself could have distinguished his own signature from my imitation of it. I am quite sure that I could not. This was, of course, entirely wrong and threw upon me a responsibility which did not belong to my office, and which I would gladly have escaped. In spite of the utmost caution on my part this fact became well-known throughout the brigade, and led the regimental officers to look upon me with additional dislike and suspicion as the power behind the throne. Of course inexperience led me into mistakes, which jealousy magnified, and for several weeks my bed was most decidedly one of thorns.

When, however, my commission as Capt. and A. A. Gen. arrived, my path

68

became considerably smoother, as I now enjoyed a rank corresponding to my position, and daily experience had taught me numerous useful lessons. From this time forward the course of my official duties became easier, and my intercourse with the regimental officers much more agreeable and cordial.

CAPTURE IN THE WILDERNESS

The advent of the spring of 1864[82] found us still encamped on the banks of Mountain Run, engaged in drill, inspections, reviews and the ordinary routine of camp life. In the happy language of Swinton[83] "Thus the months of winter glided by, till vernal grasses and flowers came to festoon the graves on battlefields over which the contending hosts had wrestled for three years. Then, upstarting, the armies faced each other along the lines of the Rapidan." I had been so busily engaged in the routine duties of my department that I had paid but little attention to the general progress of the great struggle in which we were engaged and was rather surprised than otherwise when on May 4th, 1864, we were ordered to break camp immediately, and took up once more the well-known route across Mine Run, camping about sundown at Locust Grove or Robertson's Tavern on the Orange and Fredericksburg turnpike. By sunrise the next morning we were again under arms and ready to move, and I seized the opportunity afforded by some delay in marching, to distribute to the various regiments of my brigade a number of official papers which had come to hand the preceding evening, little thinking that this was the last time I should perform that duty.

It was rumored that the enemy was in front of us, but in what force or with what precise purpose, was not known, at least to the brigade commanders. It was nearly eleven o'clock when we filed into the turnpike, and far down this road the glimmer of a brass field-piece revealed the position of the opposing forces. Advancing along the turnpike to within perhaps half a mile of the supposed position of the enemy, we turned into a woodroad leading off to the left in the direction of Germanna Ford, where we were halted to await orders. After some delay Gen. Stafford became impatient and rode back to endeavor to secure some information as to what he was expected to do, and the men seized the opportunity to take their dinner, smoke, sleep and take such ease as the circumstances admitted.

I was quietly riding along the line, reflecting upon the improvidence of

69

our superior officers in thus marching us up to the enemy without any definite orders, when some of the men who had been out into the dense undergrowth in our front returned hastily with the information that they had seen the skirmishers of the enemy advancing and not more than one hundred yards from our position. I at once called the brigade into line and was preparing to throw out skirmishers along our front, when Gen. Stafford rode up hastily and ordering us to fall back about a hundred yards from the road, formed here a new line of battle and gave the command to "Load." Immediately we advanced through the trees and bushes about a quarter of a mile, when somewhat to our right there burst forth the most tremendous roll of musketry it was ever my fortune to hear. No sound of artillery disturbed this awful roll, which gave no break nor interruption and apparently preserved for at least ten minutes an unwavering intensity. In our immediate front all was quiet save the whistle of an occasional bullet, and the solemnity of the dusky woods resounding with this terrible roll of death, which almost deafened us, and whose effects, though invisible, could readily be imagined by the veteran soldiers of our line, was far more impressive than the excitement of an active struggle.

As we advanced to the crest of a slight elevation, whose further slope was occupied by a small clearing, we were greeted by a hot fire from the enemy's line, which apparently occupied a fringe of woods at the border of the opening. Neither of our flanks was protected, although it was understood that Steuart's brigade was somewhere upon our right and the "Stonewall" brigade upon our left, though neither force was visible to us. To charge across this open field without support on either side seemed the acme of rashness, and accordingly we halted and began firing at the enemy in our front. In this position word was brought to me that the Federals were coming in upon our left flank and rear, and putting spurs to my horse I dashed off to the left, where the ride of a few rods revealed to me the skirmishers of the hostile line advancing steadily in our rear and almost upon us.

Hastily riding back to Gen. Stafford, I informed him of the situation and received his orders to throw back the left of our line at right angles to the front, so as to face the flanking force and hold them in check if possible. The First Louisiana regiment, consisting of not more than fifty men, was accordingly directed to face to the left and rear, but the Lieut. Col. commanding, instead of coolly and quietly obeying the order, seemed to lose his head entirely, and waving his sword above his head called upon his men to rally around him, which they did in a confused mass, affording little or no pro-

70

tection to our flank and furnishing an excellent target for the enemy. Deployed in a thin line, these men, if coolly handled, might at least have postponed the impending catastrophe, though I could scarcely expect them to entirely check the advance of the hostile force. Seeing no hope of accomplishing anything in the infernal uproar and confusion in this quarter, I rode back to Gen. Stafford and reported, and was then directed by him to ride quickly to the right and endeavor to find the left flank of Steuart's brigade, which should connect with our right.[84]

These were the last words ever heard by me from the unhappy General. Pushing hastily through the undergrowth in the supposed direction of Steuart's brigade, in a few moments I was surprised to almost ride over Capt. Boarman, who was lying upon the ground without arms and apparently hiding in the underbrush. To my question what he was doing there, he replied that he had been captured and had escaped, and was hiding from the enemy. I did not at the moment believe him, but feeling that there was not a moment to lose, I rode forward upon my mission as rapidly as the dense undergrowth would permit, shielding my face with one arm from the branches which threatened my eyes. Not five minutes later, as I emerged from a thicket where I was unable to see a rod ahead of me, I was thunderstruck to find myself in front of an advancing line of the enemy and not more than fifty feet from them. I had lost my way and ridden into the very arms of the Federals. The click of a dozen locks and hoarse cries of "Surrender" revealed at once the situation, and a hasty glance convinced me that escape was impossible.

A PRISONER OF WAR

As I threw down my sword in token of surrender I was roughly dragged from my saddle and marched quickly to the rear. Here I was at once disarmed of my pistol and sent in charge of two soldiers to the dêpot for prisoners near the Wilderness Tavern. On the way thither I was almost pleased to meet the courier of our staff, who had met a fate similar to my own and was likewise being conducted to the same rendezvous. "Misery loves company," and I am sure we greeted each other gladly. It must have been about 4 P.M. when we reached the dêpot for prisoners, and I was surprised to find here several hundred luckless individuals like myself, who had fallen early victims to the opening struggle. As later arrivals were drawn up in single file in order to take our names, rank, etc., a squad of hangers-on about the camps amused themselves by making witty criticisms of our clothing and personal appearance, which I doubt not would have afforded us ready entrance into the famous ragged regiment of the immortal Falstaff. After enduring this cheap wit for some time I was driven to say: "Boys! Do you think it brave and manly to insult unarmed prisoners? Before long you yourselves may occupy a similar position." Whether this had any effect I cannot say, though several of the men looked rather ashamed and the scurrility soon ceased.

In a short time we were introduced into the prisoners' pen, where, once more to my great surprise, almost the first man I met was Capt. Boarman, who had been recaptured and reached the pen before me. Soon after the Federal provost-marshall made his appearance, and asking for me presented me with a small fly-tent, which under the circumstances was a great convenience and a courtesy which I thoroughly appreciated. Just before sundown the staff-courier, who had been captured with me, and I were again summoned by an officer to Gen. Grant's headquarters, situated near by. On the way thither we learned that the object of our summons was to get from us such information of Gen. Lee's strength, purposes, etc., as we might be able and willing to give, or might let escape us through inadvertence. The courier, with rare thoughtfulness, hastily took from his pocket and tore into fragments the copies of some orders which he had recently served, and when hastily seized by our guard and handled rather roughly for his prudence, I applauded his faithfulness and protested strongly against his abuse. It would have been wiser had I imitated his thoughtfulness, for on finishing a thorough search of the courier, the guard, under orders of their officer, set at once to work to search me, in spite of my protestations against such an indignity. In my pockets were found some orders of the preceding day relating to details of drill, etc., and which I had forgotten to destroy. They were of no importance whatever, except, perhaps as revealing the number of regiments in Stafford's brigade and the names of the commanding officers, but I was greatly mortified at my carelessness in neglecting to destroy them. These papers, with the fragments of the courier's orders, were conveyed to the tent of Gen. Grant, where some sort of a council seemed to be in progress. I do not recollect, however, that any further examination of us was made, and about dusk we were reconducted to the prison-pen, where we spent our first night as prisoners-of-war.

The following morning we were marched a short distance further to the

72

rear, where we bivouacked, listening anxiously to the continued roar of musketry which told of the fierce conflict progressing in our front, and animated with hope or depressed with sorrow as the sounds of battle seemed to approach or recede.

About sundown the sharp rattle of musketry toward the Federal right, the appearance of soldiers running rapidly to the rear and the stampede of the trains in our vicinity raised us to the pinnacle of hope, and hastily snatching up our little baggage, we prepared for the deliverance which seemed now at hand. In a few moments, however, we were ordered to move from our present position, and under a strong guard took in the darkness the road toward Chancellorsville. The obscurity of the night and the forest offered abundant opportunity to individuals to escape, but the labyrinths of the Wilderness were too tangled and winding to present much hope of permanent success in avoiding the masses of the enemy by whom we were surrounded.

The next day we continued our march towards Fredericksburg, passing the Negro troops of Burnside, who gazed upon us with as much curiosity as hatred as we filed through their midst. Some of our guards had tried to frighten us by stories of the probable actions of this Negro corps when they saw us, intimating that it was extremely likely that they would massacre us on sight. I cannot say, however, that we felt greatly alarmed, and the Negroes in fact offered us little, if any, more insult than their white companions had done before. For the most part we simply eyed each other with mutual curiosity and dislike. As we progressed towards Fredericksburg our ranks were constantly augmented by new arrivals of prisoners, so that we were able to keep ourselves fairly well informed of the progress of the struggle. The body of Gen. Sedgwick,[85] killed before Spottsylvania, was borne by us on Monday the 9th, and bore silent witness that the misfortunes of war were by no means entirely on the Confederate side.

On the 13th a large body of prisoners, chiefly from Johnson's division, joined us, and from them I learned of Gen. Stafford's death from a wound received about the time of my capture. He had been shot through the body, and survived only about 24 hours in great agony. Yet he was said to have asked many questions about me, and to have expressed many apprehensions as to my fate. Indeed it was reported that I had been seen to fall wounded on the battlefield of the 5th. Poor Stafford! A braver man never lived! His friendship for me was always a mystery, since our education and natural dispositions were as diverse as possible. But in good or evil report he was alike

73

my firm and trusty friend, whose support could always be counted upon in positions of doubt and anxiety. He died as he would have chosen, on the field of battle with his face to the foe. May his soul rest in peace!

FORT DELAWARE

From the vicinity of the Wilderness we were conducted to Fredericksburg, where we took the cars to Acquia Creek and were then embarked on steamers for Fort Delaware in the Delaware river, some thirty miles below Philadelphia. We reached the fort about May 17th, 1864, and officers and men were then separated and assigned to different barracks. The latter consisted of simple wooden houses, around the interior of which wooden platforms in two tiers, like the berths of a steamer, were erected to serve as beds. The barracks were reasonably clean, and to men accustomed to the hardships of active service the hard planks of these "bunks" formed a sumptuous resting-place. Our meals were served in a long building standing by itself within the enclosure and known as the "dining-room." They consisted ordinarily of bread and coffee for breakfast, bread and meat for dinner and plain bread for supper. The food was of good quality and sufficient in quantity, and though, of course, not always tempting to a fickle appetite, was yet quite as good as the average ration of the Confederate army. The military prison was under the command of Brig. Gen'l Schoepf, and was, on the whole, well conducted and humanely administered.[86]

The leisure of the prisoners was occupied in reading, games, puzzles, etc., and after a short sojourn in my new quarters I organized a class in Latin and Greek, which afforded me congenial occupation and prevented idle repinings at my enforced quietude.[87] Soon after my arrival at Fort Delaware I wrote to Mr. E. W. Palmer of Cleveland, asking him to lend me a small sum of money for my immediate necessities, and was surprised to receive a reply from my father, who had been driven out of Tennessee by the hardships of the war in that neighborhood, and had returned a few months before to his old home in Cleveland. For three months the monotony of prison life was undisturbed by any events of importance, and rest with sufficient food had restored my strength and spirits. We were permitted to know little of the results of the campaign in progress, though enough was gleaned from contraband newspapers and chats with our guards to convince us that it had been unprecedentedly bloody and quite indecisive.

74

On August 13th, however, an officer appeared in the barracks and calling a roll of some 600 Confederate officers, directed them to prepare for immediate departure.[88] My name appeared upon this roll, and full of excitement I hastily packed up my few impedimenta and made ready to leave my quarters. The object of our removal was not stated in the order which directed its preparation, and the wildest rumors and speculations spread throughout the barracks. We were to be exchanged at once on arriving at Fortress Monroe; we were selected as victims of retaliation for certain alleged inhumanities of the Confederate authorities; we were to be simply removed to another prison, etc. All these theories were discussed over our pipes, and accepted and rejected in accordance with the varying proclivities of the hearers. Nothing, however, was known as to the real object of our removal, and with the utmost curiosity we awaited the result.

On August 20th we embarked upon the S. S. Crescent City, in the hold of which we were provided with shallow wooden "bunks," and nearly suffocated with heat and foul air. The officers of the guard, however, allowed us as much liberty in coming upon deck as was consistent with safety, and, indeed, treated us with great humanity. Fortunately the weather was fair and the sea smooth, and our ocean trip uneventful, save a narrow escape from shipwreck occasioned by the steamer running in too close to the coast and grounding off Cape Romaine on the Carolina coast.[89] A conspiracy to overpower our guards, seize the steamer and run for the Bermudas was hatching when this accident occurred, but the resulting excitement and uncertainty as to the fate of the steamer and our own safety from immediate destruction disconcerted the plot for the moment, and the appearance of a U. S. gunboat soon after on the lookout for us put an end to all hope of success. Fortunately, after several hours' delay, the steamer succeeded in extricating herself from her dangerous position, and we proceeded to Hilton Head, reaching there on August 25th.[90] Here we remained on shipboard, and on September 1st again moved up to Charleston harbor, which we reached the same day.

Considerable delay occurred off the entrance to the harbor, and it was not until Sept. 7th that we disembarked upon the southern end of Morris Island, and marching along the sandy beach by and beyond Fort Wagner, entered an enclosure some three hundred yards north of the fort and began a new phase of prison-life.[91] The enclosure or stockade was formed of pine saplings some twenty feet in length driven deeply into the sand and fastened together towards the top by horizontal braces, the whole forming an enclosure of perhaps a couple of acres. Around the outside of the stockade ran a platform for the guards, high enough for them to observe what was going on within and enabling them to command the enclosure with their guns, while about ten feet from the walls of the stockade within a stout rope was stretched, technically known as the "dead-line," beyond which no prisoner was permitted to go save at the penalty of his life. The area within the "dead-line" was laid out into six streets, flanked by simple tents for the protection of the prisoners. The latter were divided into six companies of 100 each, named A, B, C, D, E, F, assigned to their respective streets and placed under the immediate charge of a Negro sergeant, who was held responsible for the care and conduct of his company. All the guards were colored, though the commissioned officers (whom we rarely saw) were, I believe, white.

It was now apparent for what purpose we had been removed from Fort Delaware. Gen. Beauregard in Charleston had directed that certain Federal prisoners should be confined in that portion of the city of Charleston which alone could be reached by one of the Federal batteries, claiming that the bombardment of the city was in violation of the laws and usages of civilized warfare. In retaliation the Federal authorities had directed that we should be confined between forts Wagner and Gregg on Morris Island, and thus exposed to the fire of the Confederate batteries. At first glance this would seem to be a terrible position for the unfortunate prisoners of both sides. A moment's reflection, however, will recall to us the fact that no prisoners would remain in a dangerous position unless kept there by guards, and he would be a poor soldier, indeed, who could not endure with equanimity as much danger as his guards. The whole procedure was, of course, a farce, expensive and well adapted to "fire the Northern heart," but absolutely harmless to the supposed victims. Not a single prisoner was injured on either side by the fire of his friends, so far as I know, and certainly a Confederate shell rarely came near enough to our position to even excite interest.[92]

One lovely night, however, as I was sitting in the door of my tent, smoking my pipe before retiring, and watching the shells of the Confederate batteries as they rose and fell like meteors over the waters of Charleston harbor, my attention was attracted by one particular shell, apparently from Fort Moultrie, which rose to a great height and then began to descend with rapidly increasing velocity in the direction of our stockade. The colored guard in my neighborhood manifestly observed the same shell, and, halting upon his beat, gazed at it with eyes which it seemed I could almost see dilating with terror as the fiery missile approached nearer and nearer to our position. At last the shell attained a distance of perhaps a hundred yards from the stockade, when the guard, dropping his gun, fell, rather than jumped, from his platform to the sandy beach below, and grovelling upon his belly, awaited the approaching explosion. This followed at once and was perfectly harmless, though the scattering sand was driven almost to the walls of the stockade.

If, however, the exposure to the fire of our friends was harmless, the same cannot be said of the diet and the water furnished by our enemies. Our sole supply of water was procured from a shallow hole dug in the sandy beach, into which the water filtered gradually from the adjacent bay. I do not remember that it was brackish or particularly unpleasant to the taste, but it was always scanty in quantity, warm and unrefreshing. Nor was our food any better. The latter consisted chiefly of boiled rice and bean soup, the former for breakfast and the latter for dinner. The rice was usually full of worms, whose palatability was not materially improved by boiling, and this breakfast was so disgusting to me, that, by an arrangement with a comrade who preferred rice to bean soup, I exchanged my morning meal for his dinner, each of us thus omitting one meal a day, and filling up with a double ration upon the next occasion. The bread furnished was, as far as I recollect, of fair quality and quantity, nor do I remember that the small allowance of meat supplied to us was liable to severe criticism. Meanwhile the exposure to the severe heat of the sun upon this sandy beach, and the want of suitable exercise, did not contribute to render this diet any more healthful. Still most of us were young and inured to hardships and exposure by several campaigns, so that our sick-list did not become alarmingly large.

The routine of life in the stockade was monotonous enough, though not

77

entirely devoid of amusing incidents. Reveille sounded at sunrise, and we were then expected to fall into line and answer to our names at roll-call. The sergeant of my company (C), a burly Negro, good-natured and stupid, could neither read nor write, and his "roll-call" consisted in *counting* the number in his command. This was not infrequently a perplexing problem, since several men who had been already counted at one end of the line would slip quietly behind the backs of their comrades to the other end and be recounted, thus showing the presence of, perhaps, 105 prisoners instead of the 100 required. In such an event the good-natured Negro would scratch his head doubtfully, smile a feeble smile and patiently begin a recount. Now, perhaps, the movement would be reversed, and the sergeant would find his 105 prisoners shrunk to the number of only 95. Nothing, however, disturbed his imperturbable good-humor, and with a broader smile upon his round and shiny black face, he would dismiss us to our breakfasts. In the course of a few weeks we became on the best of terms with our swarthy commander, who often, when off duty, would come into our tents and chat for hours with his charges. On one of these occasions in my tent he related the story of his military experience, much to the amusement of his limited audience. It seems that he was from Boston, and, as a barber of some intelligence and means, he possessed considerable influence with his colored brethren. When the plan of raising a Negro regiment in Boston and its vicinity was broached, some of his white acquaintances persuaded him to enroll his name as a volunteer, for the sake of influencing his colored brothers, and with the understanding that he was not to be called upon for active service. When, however, the regiment was completed and organized, our worthy sergeant found, to his dismay, that this private understanding did not suffice to relieve him from active duty, and he was compelled to accompany his regiment to South Carolina. Here he had taken part in the famous assault of the 54th Mass. (colored) regiment under Col. Shaw upon Fort Wagner, July 18th, 1863, and had been wounded at the time his colonel was killed. Sent to hospital, he had recovered from his wound and been remanded to duty, but laughingly declared that if he was "lucky enough" to receive another wound the army would never see him again. Even if not particularly bright, he manifestly understood how to "play old soldier." He was always ready for a trade, and a ring of slight value that I wore upon my finger, enabled me to procure through him a number of little luxuries.

Of course our situation on Morris Island had been made known to our friends in Charleston, and a pleasant token of their remembrance and sympathy soon appeared in the donation of several hundred pounds of tobacco, which I believe was conscientiously delivered to us by the Federals. This tobacco was carefully divided by a committee of the prisoners themselves, giving to each of us a certain quantity, whether we used the weed or not. It was ludicrous to see the efforts made by some of the non-smokers to enjoy the memorial of the sympathy of their compatriots in Charleston, and I gazed with a smile upon the column of smoke which arose, like incense, from our stockade upon the night following its receipt. Thus time wore away until one evening, towards the close of October, a Federal officer appeared in the stockade and directed us to pack up our baggage at once and be ready to move at sunrise the next morning.[93] Of course visions of exchange and rumors of all sorts made their appearance promptly, and we all went to bed early to dream of "Dixie" and freedom. I was awakened just before daylight by the sound of a gun, and noticing some unaccustomed stir in the stockade, I at once arose to see what was the matter. I found that one of our officers had arisen early and made his way to the "spring" to obtain water for his morning coffee. A sleepy or stupid sentinel upon the wall of the stockade, apparently ignorant of the order for us to move at sunrise and smelling a violation of the regulations in this early riser, had fired his musket at him, but missing his aim, the ball had penetrated an adjacent tent, pierced the knapsack of a sleeping comrade and slightly wounded him in the arm. This was the only man injured during our sojourn "under fire" on Morris Island.

Snatching a hasty breakfast, we fell into line, and soon after sunrise took up our march for the southern end of the island, where after considerable delay, we embarked in a small schooner, getting on board just about sundown. Some excitement was occasioned by the effort of Capt. Coffee of Mississippi to escape under cover of the dusk of the evening by concealing himself on a neighboring vessel. He was, however, speedily discovered, and we were all crowded into the hold of the schooner, where the room was quite insufficient to permit us to lie down, the air horribly foul from crowding and lack of ventilation, and water almost unattainable. A more horrible night of feverish dreams and waking discomfort it has never been my lot to pass, and time only was required to repeat the awful crime of the infamous "Black Hole" of Calcutta. Fortunately, however, we soon arrived at our destination—Fort Pulaski—where we gladly exchanged the vile hold of the schooner for the purer air of the casemates of the fort.

Fort Pulaski, at the mouth of the Savannah River, was commanded at this period—about Nov. 20, 1864—by Col. P. P. Brown of New York,[94] a refined and educated gentleman, to whose humanity and forethought the prisoners subsequently owed many a comfort, and for whom they felt a debt of gratitude which it is a real pleasure to repay, so far as it is in my power, by a hearty acknowledgment of his kindness and humanity. Our quarters in the casemates of the fort were provided with wooden "bunks," and though often cold and uncomfortable, they contrasted so favorably with the tents of Morris Island, as to seem really palatial. At certain hours of the day we were permitted also to exercise upon a portion of the parade-ground of the fort, and for a short time our position was made as comfortable as circumstances would permit. Unfortunately the kind disposition of Col. Brown was often neutralized by the harshness of his Department commander—Gen. Q. A. Gillmore,[95] I think—whose contradictory and inhuman orders fairly wrung an apology from Col. Brown, and wrought much anxiety and injury among the prisoners. One week an order would be issued authorizing prisoners to receive money, books and articles of clothing from their friends, and promising safe delivery for all articles thus forwarded. Of course we all wrote immediately for various necessaries. The next week, perhaps, the order would be countermanded, and all donations for the comfort of the prisoners positively prohibited.

This occurred so often, and with so little apparent cause, that we were kept in a constant state of anxiety, fearing that the donations of our friends would be forwarded, and then either confiscated or lost. That this is no fancy-sketch my letters[96] of this period will abundantly prove, though of course they were written with cautious reticence. I had written to my father for a cheap edition of Herodotus to pass away the weary hours of the winter. It was sent, and reaching headquarters at Hilton Head about the time of one of these embargos, was stopped at that place, and, as I supposed, was lost. One night, however, soon after I had gone to bed and when I had fallen into a doze, I was awakened by feeling some person pulling slightly at my blanket, and turning hastily to that side I caught sight in the dim light of the casemate of a figure hastily retreating and disappearing in the darkness. Smiling to myself at the idiocy of a man who should undertake to rob me of anything valuable, I quietly turned over again and went to sleep. On arising in the morning what was my surprise to find my Herodotus tucked safely under my blanket, but with nothing to give any clue as to the route by which it had come. Of course I felt it must have been brought by my nocturnal visitor, but it was some time before I knew that the latter was the Lieut. Col. of the regiment in charge of the fort—I believe it was the 157th

N. Y. Vols. This officer was, I am told, from Syracuse, and, like Col. Brown, an educated and refined gentleman.[97] Happening to be at Hilton Head on official business, he saw my Herodotus at headquarters, and slipping it quietly into his pocket conveyed it to me anonymously and secretly—an act of generous kindness for which, I regret to say, circumstances never permitted me to return my thanks.

The monotony of our life in the casemates was not materially disturbed until January 1st, 1865, when, ostensibly in retaliation for the sufferings of Federal prisoners in the South, an order was issued cutting down the rations of Confederate prisoners to the lowest point consistent with life. No meat ration of any kind was allowed, and corn-meal was substituted for flour. To keep off the scurvy, however, kegs of pickles were rolled into the casemates and supplied *ad libitum*. As the most of us were accustomed to the use of corn-meal, the withdrawal of flour was no very serious deprivation; but the absolute denial of meat soon showed its effects upon the health of the prisoners. Col. Brown had succeeded in postponing the arrival of this order at Fort Pulaski for a week or two, and was exceedingly mortified at the necessity of enforcing it at all, but in obedience to the orders of his superiors was compelled to begin its enforcement at the date above mentioned. In the course of a month the effects of insufficient food began to show themselves in a daily increasing sick-list, which soon assumed alarming proportions. Accordingly a mass-meeting of the prisoners was held, and a committee appointed to visit Col. Brown and endeavor to effect some amelioration of our condition. Of this committee I formed one, and one Sunday evening we were conducted to Col. Brown's quarters, where we found him sitting by a cheerful grate fire, surrounded, apparently, by all the comforts of home. On stating to him the purpose of our mission, the colonel, with considerable emotion, replied substantially: "Gentlemen, I feel very sorry for you, and have done all that I could to prevent the enforcement of this order. But I am bound to obey my orders, and can do nothing for you." We then asked if he could not, at least, furnish us with sufficient lumber to enable us to partition off a portion of the casemates as a hospital, so as to enable us to separate the sick from the well. Again he replied: "Gentlemen, I can do absolutely nothing," and with heavy hearts we retired to our gloomy quarters.

Nevertheless a few days afterwards we were agreeably surprised by the appearance in our casemates of a number of barrels of fresh fish, which were rolled in quietly during the night, and rumor reported that the Lieut. Col.

81

of the post had taken a number of men with a seine, caught the welcome fish and quietly passed them into the casemates under cover of the darkness—so that Col. Brown might have no knowledge of the fact. In spite of our mournful surroundings and prospects, however, some amusing incidents served to keep us in fair spirits and to relieve the monotony of our prison-life. Col. Brown's little daughter, who with her mother shared his quarters, was the happy possessor of a beautiful white cat, which gaily decked out with a blue ribbon, was wont to sun herself upon the parade-ground, and occasionally even wandered into the casemates of the unfortunate Confederate prisoners, where she was warmly received and freely petted. Suddenly poor pussy disappeared, and no inquiries sufficed to determine the cause of her absence. About this time I was invited by some of my comrades to join them in a "swell" dinner, with the intimation that a piece of good-luck had enabled them to prepare quite a feast for the occasion. Hungry and curious, at the appointed time I joined my friends, and we sat down to an impromptu table, loaded with corn-bread, pickles and the *pièce de résistance,* an appetizing looking roast, which I took for a rabbit. To my horror, however, as the host was proceeding to carve the mysterious dish, some practical joker in the party whispered in audible tones "mee-ow" and the secret was out! The disappearance of Col. Brown's white cat was fully explained. Hungry as I was, I could not persuade myself to taste of poor pussy, though the remainder of the company ate her with apparent relish, and seemingly suffered no qualms, either of conscience or stomach.

Soon after this episode Col. Brown was relieved of the command at Fort Pulaski, whether because he was regarded as too lenient towards the Confederate prisoners, or at his own request, I have never known. He was succeeded by a Brig. Gen'l. Molyneux,[98] a little, fussy martinet, disliked cordially by the prisoners and hated, apparently, still more by the Federal soldiers of his command, who did not scruple to speak of him as a coward. About the same time, however, our prison fare was changed for one of more nourishing and healthy character,[99] so that with improving health the idiosyncrasies of our new commander, however annoying they might be temporarily, caused no permanent uneasiness. Rumors of exchange also became again prevalent and served to beguile us with the hope of at last reaching "Dixie" in earnest.[100]

Finally, sometime in March, 1865, I think it was,[101] we embarked once more and gladly bade adieu to the scene of so many trials and so much suffering. Putting in at Fortress Monroe and Norfolk, we were delayed here several days, expecting to be exchanged. Our hopes, however, were again defeated by the acute, though cruel, policy of Gen. Grant, who declared that it was cheaper to feed prisoners than to fight them. Accordingly we were once more turned back from the very portals of home, and sailed back to our old prison, Fort Delaware, which we reached some time in the latter half of March.[102] Here we met once more numbers of our old fellow-prisoners, and were also greeted by the faces of several comrades-in-arms whom the fortunes of war had brought to this prison since our departure in the preceding autumn. From the latter we learned many details of the progress of the war since our capture, and the desperate character of the struggle convinced us that the end of the war could not be far distant. Still the first reports of Lee's surrender on April 9th were discredited, and it was several days before the details of that event convinced us that the reports were, indeed, too true.

From this time the vast majority of my companions regarded the war as over, and their allegiance to the Southern Confederacy as ended. Soon after the commanding officer of the fort, under orders from Washington, called the roll of prisoners to determine how many were willing to accept their freedom, on condition of taking the oath of allegiance to the Federal government. To my disgust a large majority of my comrades decided to [accept the] offer. Personally I was not unconscious of the great temptation. I too felt confident that the surrender of Lee was the end of the Confederacy. But, so far as I knew, the Confederate government, as represented by its officials, though fugitive, still existed, and so long as this was the case, I had no excuse to forswear my allegiance thereto. The surrender of the army of Gen. Jos. E. Johnston on April 26th aggravated the situation, but still did not materially alter the facts of the case to my mind. Still, other good men concluded that it was foolish to stand longer upon punctilio, and hastened to announce their willingness to take the oath. The capture of President Davis on May 10th, however, was convincing proof of the destruction or dispersion of the Confederate government, and I now lost no time in sending in my acceptance of the new régime. Considerable delay occurred in arranging the details of the discharge of so many prisoners, and it was not until June 17th, 1865,[103] that I signed the oath of allegiance (a copy of which, with one or two Confederate notes, is preserved in my scrapbook) and was taken on a steamer to Philadelphia, where I was finally set at liberty and began fully to realize that "this cruel war is over."

United States of America.

I, *Henry E Handerson* of the County of *Rapides*, State of *Louisiana* do solemnly swear that I will support, protect and defend the Constitution and Government of the United States against all enemies, whether domestic or foreign; that I will bear true faith, allegiance and loyalty to the same, any ordinance, resolution, or laws of any State, Convention, or Legislature, to the contrary notwithstanding; and further, that I will faithfully perform all the duties which may be required of me by the laws of the United States; and I take this oath freely and voluntarily, without any mental reservation or evasion whatever.

Henry E Handerson

Subscribed and sworn to before me, at Fort Delaware, Del., this _____ day of June, A. D. 1865. _____ Capt. and A. A. A. G.

The above-named has _____ complexion, _____ hair, and _____ eyes; and is _____ feet _____ inches high.

The Oath of Allegiance sworn by Henry E. Handerson
on June 16, 1865, when he was released from Fort Delaware

More than a quarter of a century has passed over my head since the occurrences recorded in the foregoing sketch. Yet I cannot read them even now without a flush of emotion and fluttering of the heart, which testifies how real and how deep their remembrance remains in my mind. Even the blessings of peace and plenty can never obliterate the memory of the glories of a struggle, whose dearest associations are embalmed in the saddest of terms, "The Lost Cause."

Victrix causa diis placuit, sed victa Catoni. LUCAN[104]

Wartime Letters

Wartime Letters

OF HENRY E. HANDERSON
1 8 6 1 – 1 8 6 5

Alexandria, April 4th 18.61.

Dear Father,

I received yours of the fifteenth of March last Sunday and hasten to reply. I have not written as often as usual lately, being almost constantly upon the move, and being, moreover in hopes of writing something definite about my prospects. I have, however, written to Hattie[1] three or four times since my arrival in Rapides, and the fact that you have not heard from me for so long a time is due to the irregularities of the post office department. My health is very tolerable, though not as good as it was two weeks ago. I think, however, I am only a little bilious and trust that in a day or two I shall again be as bright and well as ever. I have completely broken up my chills, and weigh about my usual weight, one hundred and forty five pounds. As regards my prospects, in about two weeks I shall enter upon the situation of private teacher to the two children of Mr John Williams,[2] the same gentleman concerning whom Mr Dowe,[3] wrote to me at first. My duties will be about the same, I presume, as at Mr Compton's,[4] and my salary $500, board &c&c. I am perfectly satisfied with the arrangement and think I shall engage my services, if wanted, until a year from next October. I am very glad to receive a situation in this parish, where I have many friends, and where I shall be convenient to the City when I wish to take my remaining course of medical lectures. I am still at Gen. Graham's,[5] that is I call that my home, though I am moving about almost constantly. The Gen. has just returned from Washington City, where he has been for the last month, and I hope in a few hours to learn something reliable about political matters. There is considerable feeling here at the way in which our convention[6] has conducted itself, but I presume the people will as usual submit to what the politicians dictate. What do you think of a convention which declares that our senators and representatives

1 Superior figures refer to Notes to the Text which begin on page 131.

87

must be chosen from *members of that convention?* If that isn't impudence I dont know what is. I am sorry to hear that Pun's[7] affairs are in such confusion, but it is no more than I expected and, certainly, as he says, he has a right to do as he pleases with his own. Love to mother and Hattie, who has I suppose returned from McMinnville ere this. I will write again soon.

Your affectionate son,
Henry E. Handerson

L. Handerson Esq.

New Orleans, July 1st '61.

My Dear Father,

You will probably be much surprised to hear from me again in the city. My stay here will, however, be quite short, as on Tuesday morning we leave for "Camp Moore" on the Miss. Central R. R., about sixty miles from the city. Immediately on the receipt of your letter I enrolled myself as a volunteer in the "Stafford Guards," a company that was just leaving Rapides. This, though a hasty, was not an ill-considered step, I assure you. I had long been anxious to visit the scene of the coming struggle, and your letter, containing permission for me to offer my services if necessary, decided me. I thought that if the war was speedily ended I should soon return to my usual pursuits. And if not, my services would certainly be required, and I might be drafted into a company of total strangers. Capt. Stafford[8] himself is a warm friend of mine, and almost all my Rapides acquaintances (I mean young men of course,) are in the ranks. Young Compton[9] joins us at Camp Moore, and nearly all my most intimate friends are with me. After acquiring the drill in camp we are to leave for Virginia, and, if possible, I will make you a hasty visit as I pass through Tennessee.[10] At all events I shall have my likeness taken to-morrow,[11] and will send it to you by the first opportunity. Soldiering I find a pretty hard life, but my health is good, and to rough it for a while may be the making of me. I am delighted to see that you sympathize so warmly with the South, and, as I said before, your letter decided me to engage actively in the coming struggle. Tell mother not to let her anxiety for me prey upon her health, as I am with warm friends and true, and the same Providence that has guided me in the more peaceful pursuits of life will protect me upon the field of battle. Tell Hattie that I will write her from the camp, as I have not the time to write very much just now. Finally let me be remembered in the prayers of you all, as you are in mine. The step which I have taken is a bold one, but I trust with the blessing of God that I shall be enabled to do my duty here, as well as elsewhere in life. I will write again soon, and, with love to you all, I am

Your affectionate son,
Henry.

Direct to the "Stafford Guards," Camp
Moore, Mississippi, for the present.

My Dear Father,

I wrote you from the City that I had volunteered in the "Stafford Guards" and that we would soon leave for Virginia. I also wrote to Hattie from camp Moore in Louisiana, where we remained about a week drilling and preparing for active service. Last Thursday morning we left that camp for Virginia, and, after numerous delays, arrived here yesterday, (Wednesday), morning. Camp Hermitage is situated about a mile from the city of Richmond, at the old fair ground, and, were it not so much exposed to the sun, would be a beautiful camp ground. Whether it is really warmer here than in Louisiana I know not, but, be the reason what it may, I certainly feel the heat in Virginia much more oppressively than when I was farther south. Our company forms part of the right wing of the ninth Louisiana regiment, commanded by Col. "Dick" Taylor,[12] a son of old "Zach." Our Lieut. Col. is named Randolph, and our Major Walker.[13] It is uncertain how long we shall remain here, but, at all events, our stay will be very short;—rumor says until next Saturday. Our destination is of course known only to high officials, but the general sentiment seems to be that we shall be sent to reinforce Gen. Beauregard[14] at Manassas Gap, which will, in all probability, be the scene of the great struggle. Here, at the Capital, we know less about the war than we did in Louisiana. We are not troubled, however, with so many false and conflicting reports, and, at present, are quietly enjoying the sweets of a sundrying, which bids fair to convert us in a few days into Zouaves[15] of the most approved character. My health continues excellent, and I find that, thus far, I have stood the trials of a soldier's life far better than many men quite accustomed to "roughing it." The trip from Louisiana to Richmond was pretty severe on us all, principally from want of sleep, but I am now so used to rolling up on the ground in my blanket, or taking the soft side of a plank, (if such a luxury is attainable) that I am not quite sure that I could appreciate even a bed of down were it offered to me. Our fare is rough, but we have plenty of it, and, thus far, I have entirely escaped the various bowel complaints that afflict almost all volunteers. I ascribe my perfect immunity to my avoidance of all camp trash, and to habits as regular as this mode of life will admit. As I passed "Grand Junction" I sent my likeness to Mother, and I trust you have received it ere this. If, through God's Providence, I live to see the end of this fratricidal war, I shall try to pay you a short visit on my return to Louisiana. I suppose you know that the quondam "Bishop" Polk[16] is now a general in the Confederate army. I am sorry to see him take such a step, but I have always thought that his appearance smacked more of the sword than the mitre. By the bye, Mr. Dowe is spoken of as the chaplain of our regiment. I know he will accept if he can, and I should be delighted to welcome him once more. I have, however, very little hopes that he will be able to leave his parish. Give my warmest love to Mother and Hattie, and, trusting fully in our Heavenly Father's kind Providence, do not be over anxious. He can protect me as well on the battle field as in the more quiet walks of life. I will write you again when we make another move. Direct, for the present, to the "Stafford Guards," Richmond Va.

Henry_____

Camp Bienville, Sept. 11th '61

My Dear Father,

Yours of Aug. 26th reached me a few days ago, just when we were on the move to change our place of encampment, and I take my earliest opportunity of replying to it. Since I last wrote to Hattie we have moved on to Centerville, fairly driven out of our old encampment by its remarkable unhealthiness. Since leaving Louisiana we have lost by sickness about one hundred men, and have now some two hundred and fifty on the sick list; so you can imagine that the regiment is not in the very best fighting condition at present. My own health, however, has, with one slight exception, been excellent, contrary to the predictions of all my Rapides friends, and this rough kind of life seems to agree with me exactly, physically, albeit not so satisfactory in other respects. Typhoid fever is raging quite extensively in most of the camps, (even more so in some than in ours), but, thanks to a kind Providence, I have thus far escaped, and I trust cold weather as it advances will bring with it an entire cessation of the scourge. I fear with you that the Cleveland property is a total loss, unless, perhaps, "Pun"[17] may be able to save it, in some way, in his name. Lincoln's confiscation bill[18] I saw at the time of its proclamation, as well as the bill of our southern Congress making reparation to losing parties, but the details of both have escaped my memory and I cannot lay my hand upon either just now. If I can find the bills I will send them on to you. Your draft on New York I presume you will find at present worth no more than the paper upon which it is written. You need have no uneasiness, however, on my account. My pay, if I ever get any, will be ample for my wants and if I get none,—why I must reduce my wants to the same scale as my pay. I have some little funds now in the captain's hands, which will furnish me with some little necessaries for the winter, and, by the aid of Mother and my kind friends in Rapides, who insist upon sending me on some winter clothing, I trust I shall be able to wrestle pretty successfully with old Boreas, should the campaign last even until the spring. There will be, however, an immense amount of suffering in our camps this winter, should the war last as long as it now promises to do. Native Southerners soon sink under the inclemencies of this climate, and I fear if we are forced to endure a winter campaign here our regiment will be disbanded, and we forced into another. For this reason I think Gen. Beauregard will be inclined to hazard an engagement speedily, before the cold weather sets in, and before some of his regiments are disabled. Our pickets are now within

90

three miles of Arlington Heights and five of Washington City, and almost daily we can hear the booming of cannon which tells of a skirmish in the advance. Our regiment is now at Centerville, about twenty miles from Washington, and we hold ourselves ready to march at a moment's warning. We have already marched out twice to meet the enemy, but each time, after advancing about two miles through mud and rain, our orders were countermanded and we returned to camp. As regards the efficiency of the *equipments* of the two armies the balance is largely against us. Eight of the companies in our regiment are armed with the percussion musket and bayonet, and our own company and one other have the "Mississippi" rifle (a short large-bored weapon) without a bayonet. The northern troops have many of them Sharp's rifles and other weapons of long range, and their equipments in the battle of Manassas were of the very best quality. Perhaps the comparative inefficiency of our weapons contributes, however, to the efficiency of our troops, as it necessitates a conflict at close quarters, and a spirited charge,—the forte of southern soldiers,—often decides the fate of an action. In artillery, before the battle of Manassas, we were sadly deficient, but some sixty pieces, many of them rifled, taken in that action, have assisted us greatly. Four of our Louisiana regiments, the 6th, 7th, 8th, and 9th, are formed into a brigade with Gen. Walker[19] of Georgia as our General. He is a man of considerable experience in military affairs and we have now every confidence in him. Col. Taylor[20] is a regular martinet in the line of discipline, and aspires to have the most orderly regiment in the service. I can't say I am charmed with military life, but, as the Capt. has appointed me his book-keeper, I am excused from guard and fatigue duty, and thus escape very much of the drudgery of camp life. I am as anxious as possible to bring the war to a speedy termination, and trust that it may soon close, though the prospect certainly appears now decidedly gloomy. My place in Rapides still remains open to me when the war is over, and Mr Williams, for whom I was teaching, is now organizing a cavalry company to leave for Memphis or whatever point it is most needed. You had better direct my winter clothing to the care of Col. Richard Taylor, Manassas Junction, and mark it as plainly as possible with good *marking ink*. This address I received from the commissary of our regiment, and is, in all probability, reliable. Give my love to Mother and Hattie, and write whenever you have time.

Your affectionate son
Henry E. Handerson

Lewis Handerson Esq.

P. S. Do you know anything of the origin of the enclosed advertisement? It appeared in the "Richmond Dispatch" about a month ago and was forwarded to Col. Taylor, by whose advice I answered it giving my P. O. address, since which I have heard nothing of it.

My Dear Father,

Since I last wrote you I have passed safely through a pretty severe siege of sickness and my life is due under Providence to the kindness of Mr Dowe and Mr Newman[21] with whom I am now staying. I am still very weak and unable to walk across the room alone or even to sit up any length of time but my appetite is very good and I am gaining strength perhaps as fast as I can expect if not as fast as I could wish. I wish I had received your letter announcing the departure of my box at the time that it was written as I should have known about when to expect it. Mr Bush wrote to Manassas yesterday to inquire about it, and if it is there I shall have it sent to me here if possible. Love to Mother and Hattie and tell them to write. I will write again when I get a little stronger.

> Your son
> Henry E. Handerson

Lewis Handerson

"Camp Carondelet," Jan. 19th '62

Dear Father,

Though my letters, in consequence of very little leisure, have been few for the last month, I have yet written home considerably oftener than I have heard from there. I do not know what the reason may be, but I can testify fully to the fact that I have not received a single letter, either from home or elsewhere, since my return from Gordonsville. I wish you would all write as often as possible, for I am always anxious whenever an unusual period elapses without my hearing from you. On my return to camp some six weeks ago I found your letter of Sept. 30th awaiting my arrival. The box of clothing, Mr Dowe kindly brought to me while yet at Gordonsville, and, though I was already pretty well supplied, many of the articles I found quite useful for myself, and all will be needed by some of my fellow-soldiers. The nice woolen socks and the jeans coat were particularly serviceable, as well as the mittens and comforter. For the last month we have been busily engaged in the building and preparation of winter quarters, and are now quite comfortably fixed in our camp, about two miles east of Manassas. We have erected log cabins, which, when well daubed and finished with large fireplaces, render us as warm as we could desire. The weather thus far has been almost as mild and pleasant as in Louisiana at this season, and we have had no snow to mention. Yesterday and today, however, a cold rain has been falling, which has rendered the roads almost impassable, and quite forbids any advance of the enemy at present. On Tuesday we expect to leave for the Occoquan River, about five miles from here, in order to stand a picket guard for the ensuing six days. The prospect of a six days guard in such weather without tents or protection of any kind is not particularly pleasant I assure you though a change of most any kind is preferable to the monotony of camp life. I have thought over your suggestion of my endeavoring to secure a position in some corps of engineers, but thus far with very little result. Overlooking the difficulty of obtaining such an appointment, (for appointments now result more from favor and political influence than anything else), I think perhaps the advisability of such a course might be questioned. The war cannot in my opinion last long,—perhaps not longer than the next spring. The exertions of both parties are too tremendous to be protracted, and I do not wish to continue in the service after the present war, for which I am enlisted, is ended. I think I shall be able to graduate in Medicine after another course of lectures, and have just sent on to Richmond for some medical works to beguile the long winter evenings and brush up the knowledge which I have already acquired at some expense of time, study and money. Engineering, too, would require as much, if not more, exposure than my present life, and the pay, if the war lasts no longer than I think it will, would be of little moment. As the Capt's book-keeper I am exempt from all duties but drill, which is now merely nominal, and my pay, little as it may seem, is amply sufficient for a life where all actually necessary expenses are paid by the Government. My friends in Rapides have been urging me to procure a substitute and return to Louisiana, and at one time I thought of doing so, but I have now about made up my mind to remain "in statu quo" until the first of next May at least, trusting that a general peace will restore us all to our homes at that time. I shall certainly endeavor to visit you all when I do return, though I may perhaps find some difficulty in so doing. It is barely possible that I may obtain a furlough this winter for a short time, but this is rather improbable, as the Government seems to feel itself under no obligations of humoring the volunteers for the *war*. My health is excellent, and I believe I weigh more now than ever before in my life. The only remains of my late sickness is a head nearly bald,—a very slight matter in a place where personal appearance is so little regarded as in camp. Camp news are very scarce. We are constantly prepared for an advance of the enemy but scarcely expect it. Love to Mother and Hattie, and tell them to write as often as possible.

Your affectionate son
H. E. Handerson,

L. Handerson, Esq.

"Camp Carondelet," March 5th '62

Dear Father,

I should have written home oftener lately had not my ignorance of the extent of the successes of the Federals in western Tennessee[22] made the prudence of too frequent writing doubtful. Even now it is a doubtful question whether they have possession of the city of Nashville, though we presume that they have, and I wish you would inform me when a correspondence with home by the usual mail routes becomes unsafe. As it now seems very possible that you may be again subjected, at least for a time, to the Lincoln rule, you must not be surprised or alarmed if my letters should be less frequent than heretofore. Perhaps I may manage to get one through the blockade occasionally, but, as the revelation of my whereabouts might be seriously detrimental to your interests, I shall endeavor to be as cautious as possible. Any alarm on my account would, however, be misplaced. Providence will protect me in the future, I trust, as in the past, and, should anything untoward befall me, I will take measures to acquaint you with it as soon as possible. I hope, however, all this may be unnecessary caution, and that the South, aroused from her torpidity by her recent reverses, may arise in her strength and expel the invader from every foot of her territory. Your uncertainty as to my P. O. address was very natural, though entirely overlooked on my part. The various camps at which my letters were dated have all been situated in the neighborhood of Manassas, which has always been, and still continues to be my post-office. Should my address be changed, (as seems very possible now), I will let you know as early as possible. E. G. Randolph is the name of our present Col., vice R. Taylor, promoted to Brigadier General. We have been anticipating an attack from Gen. McClellan every day for the past week, but to all appearances this is as far distant now as ever. Perhaps, however, fear that the star of Buell,[23] now rising in the west, may eclipse ere long his own brightness, may urge him on to a more speedy movement than his programme seemed to foreshadow. If so I trust we shall be able to give him a warm reception, and to retrieve the losses of forts Henry and Donelson.[24] By the way Capt. J. Routh Williams, (the gentleman for whom I was teaching when the war broke out), is somewhere in western Tennessee, at the head of a cavalry company, and, if it is in your power to extend him any little courtesies, I wish you would do so for my sake. Enclosed I send you Senator Trumbull's bill[25] confiscating the property of rebels and those abetting the rebellion. Whether it has ever been passed I do not know. I wish you would send me the letter from young Goodrich as soon as convenient. Perhaps I may be able to assist him, and, if so, I should like to do so. Love to Mother & Hattie, and ask them to write often. My health is tolerable and improving.

Your affectionate son,
H. E. Handerson.

Lewis Handerson Esq.

Camp—Near Richmond, Va. July 12th 1862

Dear Father,

I received yours of June 26th two days ago but reached this Camp so completely prostrated by fatigue that I was unable to answer it immediately as I wished to

94

do. I am pretty nearly recovered now, and a few days of rest will undoubtedly restore me to my usual health. Our regiment was with Jackson throughout his famous valley campaign, did good service there, crossed over to the rear of McClellan's forces before Richmond and participated in the two bloodiest of the series of battles around that city,—that of Gaines' Mills or Beaver Dam and Malvern Hill. In all these conflicts I have escaped unharmed though a Minié ball ruined my hat in the battle of the 27th. McClellan was undoubtedly defeated before Richmond but the result has not been as decisive as we had all hoped, nor as it would have been had our generals *all* obeyed orders. Some months however must elapse before the Federals will be able to renew offensive operations. McClellan is now about 30 miles from Richmond on the James river, under the protection of his gunboats, and awaiting reinforcements. His loss will reach nearly 30,000 men and stores incalculable. Ours is estimated as high as 15,000. I will write more fully in a few days—tomorrow if possible. Love to Mother and Hattie.

Your Son
H. E. Handerson

L. Handerson Esq.

Camp—, near Richmond, Va, July 13th '62

Dear Father,

I wrote you a few lines yesterday to relieve you of all anxiety on my account, but had to defer a full account of my proceedings since the evacuation of Manassas to a period of more leisure. Immediately upon the evacuation of that position, we retreated by forced marches to the line of the Rappahannock, and thence, after a sojourn of some three or four weeks, to Gordonsville. From this place we proceeded, via Stanardsville, to the valley of the Shenandoah, where we joined Gen. Jackson, and bore our full part in the dangers and glories of his famous valley campaign. You have doubtless read many accounts of our successes in this portion of Virginia, but the story of my experience may not be uninteresting. Having joined Jackson's forces near Harrisonburg, we advanced with all speed towards Front Royal, where was stationed a small portion of Banks' division. Our appearance there was a complete surprise. The town was carried at the point of the bayonet, and almost the whole of the 1st Maryland (Federal) regiment captured, with an immense amount of army stores. The only item that renders this action memorable to me is that in it I fired my first shot at the enemy. I can, however, say safely that, if my shooting since has not improved upon my first shot, my conscience is free from every stain of blood. The only visible effect was a slight acceleration of a gait already headlong. In Yankee parlance my man "skedaddled." This was on May 23^d. On the 24th we advanced on the road towards Strasburg as far as Middletown, where we again met the enemy, and, after a sharp fight, completely routed them, taking many prisoners and many more army supplies. Our company whose duty as skirmishers throws them in advance of the whole army, (not always, however, but when their *turn* comes to skirmish), was engaged from about 11 A.M. until after sundown, when we were obliged to rejoin our regiment. This broke us all down, and we were ordered to halt some five miles from Winchester, while the other troops advanced and, after a short but bloody struggle, took that city. From this place we went on to Harper's Ferry, took a longing look into Maryland, and reluctantly began our retreat up the valley, to avoid being cut off by Fremont and Shields, who were advancing upon our rear. Had these two generals formed a junction we should have been completely trapped, and I should have been enjoying now the hospitalities of Fort Warren[26] or some other stronghold. Jackson, however, outwitted both. Sunday, June 8th, he met Fremont. The battle was long and bloody, and at sunset both parties rested on the field of battle. During the night, however, Jackson withdrew his forces across the Shenandoah by the bridge at Port Republic, and, early Monday morning, came thundering down upon Shields, who, during the whole of the same night, had been sending over reinforcements to assist Fremont in the supposed battle of the morrow. Shields fought well, but by noon was badly whipped, and in full retreat, while Fremont, on the other side of the river, could only look on and gnash his teeth at the slaughter which he could not prevent. Jackson had burned the bridge after crossing. But my story is getting too long. From the Valley we came via Charlottesville, Gordonsville &c upon the rear of McClellan's right wing, caught him too napping, and participated in the engagements of Gaines' Mills or Beaver Dam and Malvern Hill. It is useless to describe these actions, except to say that the intensity of the fire far exceeded all that we had experienced in the Valley. In the former action (Gaines' Mills,) four of my companions fell dead, and four severely wounded, within ten steps of me, in the short space of fifteen minutes, while I escaped with a bullet hole in my hat. Strange to say, from the position in which our regiment was placed not a single one of the enemy was visible, being concealed behind a breastwork of logs, hidden by the dense foliage of the Chickahominy swamps. We fired only at the smoke of their guns. To conclude a long description of scenes at which you doubtless shudder, let me say that McClellan was forced to retreat at every point, and fell back to a point on the James river about 25 miles from Richmond, and now rests under the protection of his gunboats, with which we have nothing at present able to cope. His defeat is not so decisive as we had hoped to make it, but it has proved, at least, a most serious reverse, and will incapacitate McClellan from any further "on to Richmond" movements for three months to come. I was overjoyed to hear from home once more, and I hope communication will never be interrupted between us again. Perhaps, if the war is not concluded before next winter, I may be able to obtain a furlough and come on to see you

96

all, but none can tell what a month may bring forth. Do you ever hear anything now from "Pun"? On the borders, as it were, of two great republics perhaps you can communicate with both. Write as often as possible and I will do the same.

Your affectionate son,
Henry E. Handerson

Lewis Handerson Esq.

I shall try to get into Richmond tomorrow and call on Mr. O. P. Baldwin.

[*Added to previous letter*]

Dear Sister,

I received a letter a few days ago from you, dated March 25th. Did it come by way of China? At least, it was almost as welcome as a visitor from the celestial empire. That it is dull and monotonous at home is easily imagined. It is so everywhere, and, particularly, in camp. You ask what I find to do. I answer, Write! Write! Write! from morning till night. I have been detailed as clerk in the Q. M. department ever since we left Gordonsville, though I have rather neglected my business in this line to see a little active war. Perhaps it was a tempting of Providence, but, for once, my curiosity overcame my discretion. The experience of five bloody battles has, however, pretty well satisfied my curiosity, and I feel deeply grateful to a kind Providence for protection in hardships and dangers innumerable. What do you think of *four* hard crackers and half a pound of pickled pork as food for a day? I have lived many a day on nothing else; the pork too I have often eaten *raw*, fires being prohibited in presence of the enemy. From Sunday noon June 8th until Monday night at sundown I ate nothing but some raw corn, that I stole from the horses of the wagon yard. You can imagine the visions of Mother's pumpkin pies and other dainties that visited me in my troubled dreams. So you preside now at the wash tub do you? I have done that for some time, though I can't claim much spotless linen as my handiwork. Love to Mother, and tell her that I will, hereafter, run into no dangers unnecessarily, and hope to see you all yet in peace and quiet. Write just as often as possible.

Your brother
Henry.

Direct for the present to Richmond.

"Ashby's Gap," Loudon Co., Va. Sept. 6th 1862.

Dear Father,

I presume you have heard ere this of the battles at Manassas and in that vicinity and I write to let you know of my safety and continued welfare. You need, however, feel no anxiety concerning me at present as my duties in the Q. M.

Department keep me always in the rear of the army and during the late battles I was some forty or fifty miles from the scene of conflict. Even now we have not overtaken Jackson's division to which we are attached and do not really know where it is though rumor reports it at Leesburg. Of the details of the late battles we know as yet very little. Our victory though decisive has been most bloody and the Federals are reported to have fought with the utmost desperation. In my own company a long list of twenty one killed and wounded, (more than one half of those present,) attests that they did their duty. A story told of the Louisiana brigade and attested as true by the Adjutant of our regiment will show at least the desperation with which *this* brigade fought. They were assailed by *five* Federal brigades in succession and when their ammunition failed continued to fight with rocks, and incredible as it may seem succeeded in holding their position until again supplied when they speedily put the Yankees to the rout. We have had no very late news from the army but it is rumored that Pope and his whole forces have retired beyond the Potomac, resolved I presume to make one last desperate stand for the defence of Washington. I do not however credit the rumor. Pope though defeated has still a large force under his command and reinforcements are continually pouring in to him. I do believe, however, that our Generals intend to "carry the war into Africa" and Stuart's[27] cavalry are reported already in Maryland. If this be true Washington may fall before the echo of "On to Richmond" has left our ears. We hear rumors too of decisive advantages gained by Bragg[28] in the Mississippi valley, of the recapture of Nashville and fort Donelson and the evacuation of New Orleans by the brute Butler,[29] but the news is I fear too good to be true. If, however, these tidings are confirmed the Federals will have the satisfaction of finding themselves at the close of the present campaign worse off by thousands of men and hundreds of millions of money than at its outset, and no important successes to balance this ruinous account. I trust the season of Winter and the necessary cessation of active hostilities may give them time for reflection and that peace counsels may hereafter have some voice and weight in controlling the steps of the northern Government.

Did you ever receive the two letters that I wrote you from Richmond? Having heard nothing from you since, I fear they may have miscarried, though I directed them precisely as you told me. How is mother's health now? Better I trust than when Hattie last wrote me. Give my love to them both and ask them both to write whenever an opportunity presents itself. Write yourself too as often as possible.

Your son
H. E. Handerson

L. Handerson Esq.

Sept. 10th Jackson, Ewell, Longstreet, Hill and other generals are now in Maryland with their respective divisions. Numerous riots are reported in Baltimore. Perhaps the beginning of the end is even now at hand.

Have just received Hattie's letter of August 8th and will write to her in a few days. We started through the gap the day before yesterday, but being waylaid by some Yankee cavalry and an attack threatened we were obliged to return to this place with our whole train. For a few hours our danger seemed imminent, but some 150 of us having found some old muskets in the wagons, and bringing up a six-pound rifled cannon that by good fortune happened to be in the rear of the train, presented so warlike an appearance that the Yankees concluded "discretion the better part of valor." Had they attacked when first seen our whole train, worth probably at least a million of dollars, would have fallen an easy prey.

Winchester, Va, Sept. 16th. Harper's Ferry was taken yesterday, report says with 15000 (?) Federal prisoners.[30]

Camp—near Front Royal, Va. Nov. 6th '62

Dear Father,

I wrote to Hattie some two weeks ago communicating all the news of importance that I could think of, but as I have now a few moments of leisure I thought I would let you know of my continued health and welfare. When I last wrote I believe I had rejoined my company in the 9th Regiment. About a week ago, however, in the absence of the regimental Quarter Master I was detailed by Col. Stafford to perform his duties and find myself thus once again in the Q. M. Department. Our corps of the army has not been in any engagement since the Sharpsburg affair, though we hear the roaring of cannon and rumors of fierce battles beyond the mountains almost daily. No decisive engagement has taken place, however, so far as I know. Yankees are reported around us in all directions but Jackson is so much at home in the Valley that we have no fear for the result. We have all been wonderfully mystified at Bragg's[31] movements in Kentucky and hardly know whether to call him victor or vanquished. Can you tell me what he has *done* in this wonderful campaign of his? I said above that we had been in no engagement lately. You must not imagine, however, that we have been idle. Some ten or fifteen miles of the Baltimore and Ohio R. R. torn up and destroyed bears witness to our industry. Verily I never thought I should ever become such a "bridge-burner"! Yesterday an order was sent to Brig. Gen. Hays,[32] (a brother of the ranger Hays[33] of Texan notoriety), for his "crack" regiment to perform most dangerous service. The Ninth was sent, every man prepared to wade through seas of blood, when behold not a Yankee appeared to bar their peaceful progress

99

and they returned to camp last night sound in every thing but the feet, blistered by a long days march. Such is war!

I had a letter from Rev. Mr. Dowe a few days ago but it contained no particular news. All the necessaries of life are scarce and high but the planters are in usually good spirits. Prices in this country are most exorbitant. A very common suit of clothes costs in Richmond from fifty to seventy-five dollars, and other things in proportion. Richmond is reported in great excitement at present, in consequence of the prospect of a speedy recognition of the Confederacy by France and England. This old cry seems to rise from its ashes almost monthly. I have no more faith in it.

The report of cannon, usually a premonitory symptom of a speedy movement on our part, warns me to close. Write often and direct to Richmond, as before. Love to Mother & Hattie.

Your son
Henry E. Handerson

Lewis Handerson Esq

Camp of "Hays' Brigade" near Front Royal, Va. Jan. 14th '63

Dear Father,

Your last letter has remained unanswered much longer than I either wished or intended. I wrote you, however, soon after the battle of Fredericksburg, informing you of my continued safety and health, but, as I directed the letter to McMinnville,[34] it may never reach you. Bragg's late victory (?) and flight has again exercised us considerably. We know not what to think of him, and after his boastful dispatches but little corroborated by subsequent movements I am beginning to be very distrustful of his capacity. Our cause surely needs no such lame assistance as lying dispatches, and an honest avowal of defeat is not near so painful to me as a mere paper victory. Perhaps, however, I do Bragg injustice, but his victories are at least peculiar to himself. Lee presents a most decided contrast, and his official dispatch regarding the battle of Fredericksburg, probably the most disastrous defeat that the Federals have suffered since the first Manassas, is a model of modesty and truth. Since that battle we have had nothing to do but watch the enemy, our pickets on one bank of the Rappahannock and theirs on the other, about eight hundred yards apart. No firing is allowed on either side, and we frequently have friendly chats and interchanges of papers, tobacco and coffee. Since the 1st of January, however, I have been again assigned to duty in the Q. M. Department. You will, probably, think me very changeable, but this change was not entirely voluntary on my part. Capt. Hughes our regimental Q. M. was sick, and flattered me enough to say that he thought me better able to attend to his business, during his absence on furlough, than any other available officer in the

100

regiment. In proof of this, I suppose, he left me an enormous legacy of half finished accounts, with orders to make his returns to the Department as soon as possible. Consequently I have been up to my ears in invoices, abstracts &c for about two weeks and just begin to see my way out. I regret the change for two reasons, one, that by shifting about from the line to the Q. M. Department I get a smattering of my duties in both places without knowing much of either, and the other, that I fear I have lost all chance of a furlough this winter by leaving my company.

Jan. 18ᵗʰ 1863

For the last two days we have been under marching orders in anticipation of another advance of the enemy, who are said to have completed two bridges across the river above our position. I doubt both the fact and the inference, however, and am inclined to think the movement a mere feint to engage our attention here, and cover far more serious designs in North Carolina. If the excitement wears away soon, and Capt. Hughes relieves me from my present position, I think I shall apply for a short furlough, in which case, I hope to pay you a visit sometime in March. At all events, I wish you would let me know whether communication is open between Chattanooga and McMinnville, in your next letter, or where I had better leave the R. R. Tell Mother I have now plenty of socks & clothes of all kinds, as the ladies of Rapides parish, La. have remembered us all bountifully this winter. I will write as often as I can find time, but you must expect broken & disconnected letters for the present, as I am liable to interruption at every moment. With love to Mother & Hattie, whose last letter though unanswered is not forgotten, I am.

Your Son
Henry

Hospital No. 10. Richmond, Va. May 13ᵗʰ '63

Dear Father,

You will, doubtless, be surprised at the heading of my letter, supposing me with the army upon the Rappahannock. There I should be, had it not been for a more intimate acquaintance with Yankee lead than was at all pleasant or convenient. To speak plainly, I am now recovering from the effects of a slight wound, received in the late battles on the line of the Rappahannock. The wound, (in my neck), is, however, doing finely, and I expect to be able to report for duty again in two or three weeks. On Wednesday, April 29ᵗʰ, we were all aroused from our beds by the roll of musketry at no great distance, and, on inquiring the cause, found that the Yankees were really crossing the river in heavy force. We immediately formed line of battle and marched out to meet them. Heavy skirmishing ensued in our immediate front, but no decisive battle, as the crossing here was, as yet, but a feint. Meanwhile, Hooker, with a force of some 120,000 men, was crossing the river about fifteen miles above, intending to pass our left flank and take position in our rear. As soon as his design was disclosed, all our troops, except our division, (Early's), were ordered up the river to check Hooker, while we were left to hold the heights around Fredericksburg. In our immediate front was the Yankee Gen. Sedgwick with his corps, (three divisions), of 30000 men, to oppose which we had, at the utmost, not more than Early's division and Barksdale's brigade, not exceeding 12000 in all. We were not attacked, however, until Sunday morning, May 3^d, when, after some heavy fighting, our center was broken by a heavy column of the enemy, and we were compelled to fall back some three miles, which we did in good order, our brigade, which was on the extreme left, suffering very little. On Monday we were reinforced by the divisions of Anderson and McLaws, which had assisted in the defeat of Hooker in the battles of "The Wilderness" and Chancellorsville, and, late Monday afternoon, our brigade, having passed around the right of the enemy, drew up in line of battle in their rear. At six P. M. the signal sounded for the attack, and with such a cheer as Louisianians alone can give we charged the enemy in a full run. Such a scene as ensued never entered into my imagination. Right in front of us was a battery, supported by heavy masses of infantry. On our right and left the same,— a wall of fire on three sides. The air was fairly hissing with round shot, shell, grape, canister and minié balls. There was no time, however, for hesitation, and on we rushed, carrying every thing before us. For about a mile we swept everything in our track, two of the batteries galloping off to avoid capture. Finally, however, owing to the rapidity of our charge, the brigade became inextricably confused. One half the men were so broken down by previous hard marching as to be unable to keep up with the rest. Officers lost their companies, and companies their officers. Regiments had no commanders. No support was near us, and fresh bodies of the enemy flanking us on the right. We were ordered to fall back and reform. Now came the pinch. "Facile descensus Averni &c" Virgil says; which may be freely interpreted, "It . . . [pages 5–8 missing; page 9 continues] at the point where the brigade was to be reformed, I set to work to assist in the reorganization. Lieut. Bringhurst, however, saw the hole in my coat, and advised me to go to the hospital, which I did, as my right shoulder was growing very stiff and painful. On examination the ball was found to have entered on the back of my neck, and, passing around lodged among the muscles just over the carotid artery. One half an inch more would infallibly have cut my throat. Our surgeon extracted the ball very skillfully and neatly, and the wound is now healing rapidly. It has given me very little pain, and I have every reason to thank Providence for so easy an escape from such imminent danger. Thus ended my share of the grand "charge of Hays' Brigade", which, though not a complete success, was mainly instrumental in driving the Yankees back across the river at Fredericksburg. Gen.

Lee, I understand, compliments us very highly, and, indeed, it was a brilliant affair, only marred, in my opinion, by the fault of our Brig. Gen. Hays, who should never have allowed us to charge in a full run. Some of the scenes appear to me almost ridiculous, as would the whole affair, had I not to mourn the loss of many friends. Capt. Cummings' (my captain,) was killed on the field, together with five of his men. Nine of us were wounded, of whom four lost their limbs. Col. Stafford is missing, as well as Major Williams, who was by me in the ditch. Both are probably prisoners. The total loss of the brigade is 663, or about one third of those who went into action. Hooker's defeat above was also complete, though, perhaps, more than compensated by the loss of Gen. Jackson, who died of his wounds a few days ago. He had been outside of our lines on a reconnaissance, and returning with his staff after dark, was mistaken for an enemy and fired upon by his own men. His left arm had to be amputated, but he was doing finely, when pneumonia set in, and finally overcame him. We could better have spared 50000 men. On the Rappahannock matters remain just as before the fight; the enemy on the north bank, and we on the south. Another advance is, however, expected soon. We shall be ready to meet it. What is the prospect in Tennessee? Do you anticipate any collision there immediately? I see the Yankee cavalry have been to McMinnville since I left there, burning the cotton factory &c. Did they venture as far as Beersheba? How is your hand now? I have not heard one word from home since I left you, and am very anxious to hear from you.[35] You can direct as heretofore to the regiment, as I shall probably be back there almost as soon as this reaches you. Tell Mother to feel no anxiety about my wound, as it could not be doing better. Mrs. Greenhow,[36] of northern prison celebrity, has been my nurse, and has taken excellent care of me. Remember me to all friends and, tell Hattie to write often.

Your Son
H. E. Handerson

To.
Lewis Handerson Esq.
  Beersheba Springs,
    Tenn.

Officers' Barracks, Fort Delaware,
June 13th 1864.

Dear Father,

    Yours of the 4th inst. was duly received. I am delighted to hear once again from home folks, and to know that you are all as well as usual. The box of clothing and the money were both received and their receipt was acknowledged immediately to Mr. Palmer.[37] Glad as I should be to see you, I do not think you could add materially to my comfort by a visit. I am quite as comfortably situated as I had anticipated, and have very little to complain of as regards my treatment. I enclose a copy of the regulations of Brig. Gen'l Schoepf relative to interviews with, and the correspondence of, prisoners of war. If you can manage to send me a little money monthly for current expenses I shall be able to make out tolerably well until exchanged, and this is about all that can be done for my comfort. Ask Mother and Hattie to write as often as possible. All letters of a private character will, probably, be safely delivered. Tell uncle Eph.[38] I have returned again to my first love, and am now deep in the mysteries of Caesar and Xenophon. With love to Mother, Hattie and aunt Esther, I am

Your Son

Henry E. Handerson

L. Handerson Esq.

Officers' Barracks, Fort Delaware,

August 13th 1864.

Dear Father,

I have just been chosen to be sent to Hilton Head,[39]—whether for retaliatory measures or for exchange I cannot say. There is a fair prospect, however, of the latter. I will write again by the first opportunity and, should I be fortunate enough to reach "Dixie" in safety, will write by the first flag of truce boat. I will try to return the books which you recently forwarded to me, but doubt whether I shall be successful. With love to Mother, Hattie and all friends I am,

Your Son

Henry E. Handerson

L. Handerson Esq.
  Cleveland,
    Ohio

Officers' Barracks, Fort Delaware,

August 14th 1864.

Dear Father,

I have just received your letter of the 9th inst. enclosing $10.00. I wrote yesterday stating that I was one of 600 Confed. Officers to be sent to Hilton Head. I am expecting to leave every moment. There is little doubt now that we shall be exchanged on our arrival at Charleston. So you need feel no extraordinary anxiety concerning me. Most of the books I shall be able to carry with me. The remaining few I have given to friends. It was impossible to have them sent back.

104

I had hoped that Mother's health was entirely restored. Do not let her worry herself about me, as I am in excellent health and spirits and hope to be soon again at my post. Love to all.

Your Son
Henry E. Handerson

I will try to write by flag of truce as often as possible.

Officers' Barracks, Fort Delaware,
August 18th 1864.

Dear Father,

I have been expecting hourly to leave here every day for the last five days, but am still in statu quo. We have numerous rumors relative to the delay of our departure, none of which are worth notice. It is probable, however, that we shall leave here at some time during the present week. Hilton Head is stated to be our destination, but even this is by no means certain, and what is the object of our removal is unknown. I hope, however, it may eventually result in an exchange. Your letter enclosing $10.00 was duly received and its receipt acknowledged on the 14th inst. I have heard nothing from the missing box, and, if the Express Agt succeeds in finding it, I presume you had better have it returned to you at once. I hoped to be able to send you my photograph before leaving, but will send it by flag of truce from Richmond, if I should be fortunate enough to reach there soon. I will also endeavor to write as often as possible. Should we not leave this prison at all, (a by no means impossible contingency) I will bear in mind the instructions relative to clothing &c contained in your last letter. An order has been issued recently here prohibiting prisoners from corresponding with persons other than their father, mother, brother, sister or wife. This will prove very severe on those who have no near relatives in the *North,* and I am very glad that I am among the fortunate few who are at least permitted to write. I hope Mother's health continues to improve, and I think a restoration to Church privileges will prove a valuable sanitary agent in her case. Remember me kindly to Dr Berry,[40] for whom I have more respect and affection than for any minister in the world. I had intended to write to Hattie, who is now I presume at Orange, but have been prevented by the scarcity of postage stamps. My health continues good and under the prospect of an exchange my spirits are most exuberant. I heard indirectly from Rev. Dr Perry[41] and his worthy son a few days ago. The latter has become a minister of the Gospel and attained some rather unenviable notoriety. Love to Mother, Hattie, aunt Esther, the uncles P. and all friends.

Your Son
Henry E. Handerson

L. Handerson Esq.

C. S. Officers' Quarters, Morris Island, S. C.
September 8th 1864

Dear Father,

We left Fort Delaware on the 20th ult. on the U. S. steam-ship Crescent and reached Hilton Head on the 25th. Our trip was pleasant, so far as the weather is concerned, but with 600 officers crowded into the hold of a single ship you can imagine that our position was anything but comfortable. We arrived at Hilton Head without serious accident, however, although narrowly escaping shipwreck by running onto Cape Romaine on the N. C. coast. We remained on shipboard at Hilton Head until the first inst., when we sailed for Charleston harbor, arriving here the same day, but were not disembarked until yesterday. We are now quartered just between batteries Wagner and Gregg on Morris Island and in plain view of Charleston, distant some 3 or 4 miles. A constant cannonade is kept up between these batteries and the Confederate batteries in the vicinity of the city, but up to this time, no shells from our batteries have fallen very near us,—probably none nearer than a quarter of a mile. I presume the Confed. authorities have been informed of our position and take pains to avoid it. Though our situation is by no means comfortable it is so far superior to that on shipboard that we are almost happy. On the ship we all suffered intensely from bad air and scarcity of water. My health still holds out bravely, however, and I hope yet to weather all these hardships and reach "Dixie" at last. There is no prospect of an immediate exchange, but hope has by no means deserted us. We are allowed to correspond with friends in both "Dixie" & the U. S. under similar regulations to those at Fort Delaware. My address is "Prisoner of War, Morris Island, S. C." Love to Mother and Hattie and tell them to feel as little anxiety about me as possible.

Your Son
Henry E. Handerson

L. Handerson Esq.
Cleveland,
Ohio

Fort Pulaski, Georgia,
October 30th 1864

Dear Father,

Yours of the 10th inst. enclosing $5.00 in "greenbacks" reached me safely on the 28th. I had previously written to Hattie informing her of our removal from Morris Island to this place, where we arrived about a week ago. Our situation now is much improved in every respect. Our rations are sufficient in quantity and very fair in quality. My long continuance on the same diet, however, threatens me with the Scurvy, and I have invested a portion of the funds in pickles to try and overcome a sore mouth which is troubling me considerably. With the exception of this sore mouth and an intolerable cold occasioned by our transfer from tents to closer quarters in the casemates of this fort my health is very good. I see no prospect of any exchange which will affect us, and am endeavoring to resign myself with as good grace as I can muster to the idea of spending my winter in this place. I wish you would send me by mail a copy of Herodotus, (Leipsic edition, cheap paper cover), as soon as convenient. Any funds forwarded as were the last will be pretty certain to reach me safely. You speak of having enclosed also some postage stamps in your last letter. None were enclosed when it reached me, and, as it is very difficult to procure them here, I wish you would send more in your next. Fasten them to the paper to avoid their loss. With love to mother and Hattie, and the hope of hearing from you soon I am

Your Son
Henry E. Handerson

L. Handerson Esq.

Fort Pulaski, Ga. November 27th 1864.

My dear Sister:

Your letter of the 1st inst. reached me safely two days ago. I have also received two other letters from you and two from Papa since I left Fort Delaware. One of the latter contained $5.00, the receipt of which was acknowledged immediately. I have also written to you once or twice since my arrival at this fort, but our mail facilities are so irregular that it does not surprise me to learn you have not received these letters. Do write as often as possible, however, for your letters always occasion me great enjoyment, and I shall probably receive them after some delay. Tell Papa, however, to send no more money as an embargo has been placed upon all moneyed letters, packages of clothing &c forwarded to prisoners of war at this place. Some real or fancied wrong by the Confederate officials in the Dept. of Georgia is assigned as the reason of this deprivation. Enclose a stamp in all your letters as I shall soon be unable to procure any here. My health continues good and our condition is much improved by our removal from Morris Island. We have suffered somewhat from cold since our arrival here, but I am far better provided with underclothing than many of my unfortunate fellow prisoners & do not intend to complain. I see no prospect of our exchange & in fact have almost ceased to expect it or even to think about it. Consequently I am endeavoring to reconcile myself to a continued residence in Northern prisons, and hope, by the aid of a few books, to at least preserve myself from insanity. Do not neglect to write often and let me know all the news relative to our friends. Am very sorry

to learn of Mrs. Rose's illness. What has become of our pretty little "Mamy"?
Love to Papa, Mother and all friends.

Your brother

H. E. Handerson

Fort Pulaski, Ga. December 4th 1864

Dear Father,

I wrote to Hattie last Sunday and requested her to say to you that an embargo
had been placed upon all boxes etc. forwarded to prisoners in this Dept., and to
warn you not to forward anything to me. This embargo has proved merely temporary and is now removed, and, should any hindrance be placed in future on
the receipt of packages from our friends, I presume it will not be permanent. I
wish therefore that you would send me by mail or otherwise the copy of Herodotus for which I wrote when on Morris Island, together with a similar copy of
Tacitus, (History, Annals, Germania & Agricola). The Leipsic edition, (by
Tauchnitz), or the Oxford, either of which is both good & cheap will answer my
purpose perfectly well, and may easily be sent by mail. I am also getting into a
bad condition as regards outer clothing and enclose my measure for a suit of
clothes. If the Express Company will engage to deliver them to the commandant
of this post, Col. P. P. Brown, it will doubtless be best for you to procure them in
Cleveland and forward them; but if not, I presume I shall be obliged to call
upon you for money enough to purchase them of the sutler at this post. If purchased here they will cost, I presume, about $50.00. What I need is of course
something *serviceable* not elegant;—a plain frock-coat, vest and pants. If you
conclude to purchase the clothing yourself please send also a good blanket, dark-
colored. My health continues good, and our treatment is as good as we could
expect,—excellent when compared with that of Morris Island. Do write as often
as possible, and enclose some stamps in your letters, as it is very difficult to procure them here. Love to Mother and Hattie, for whose safety and comfort I am
more than thankful. Direct packages to "Care of Col. P. P. Brown, Comd'g Post.

Your Son

Henry E. Handerson

L. Handerson Esq.

Fort Pulaski, Georgia, December 14th 1864.

Dear Father,

Yours of the 23^d ult., (through politeness of Col. Brown), reached me on the
12th, and I hasten to acknowledge the receipt of the $10.00 therein enclosed. I
also received on the same day Hattie's letter of th 3^d ult. enclosing some postage

stamps. If you have not heard from me frequently since my arrival at Fort Pulaski it has been owing to causes over which I can have no control. I have written at least once every week since I came here, acknowledging the receipt of all letters up to date. I had no idea that it would require so much trouble on your part to procure the copies of Herodotus and Tacitus for which I wrote. They ought to be in any book store, especially in the cheap editions which I desired. However when once procured they will last a long time, and will, I trust serve to while away many an hour of the long & tedious term of imprisonment to which I look forward. We are constantly tantalized with rumors of exchange but I see nothing whatever upon which to found a belief in such an event. Everything points to another four years of horror & of blood. Our quarters are probably fixed permanently enough for you to send anything to me, but I would not advise you to send me eatables of any kind. Col. Brown promises to deliver all packages for prisoners unless prevented by orders from superior H^d Qrs., but eatables of all kinds are so likely to spoil in transit, that you had better avoid them. I can purchase pickles, onions &c here in sufficient quantities to keep off the scurvy, of which I am now almost free. Should Capt. Culp volunteer to deliver the clothing for which I wrote some time ago, you can accept his services, *but do not ask him to do so.* I prefer rags. My general health is good, and spirits as equable as usual. Love to all friends,

Henry E. Handerson

L. Handerson Esq.

Fort Pulaski, Geo. Jan'y 10th 1865

Dear Father,

I have been delaying writing to you for some time in the hope that I might be soon able to communicate something cheerful relative to our condition and prospects. I see no prospect, however, at present of any improvement in the regulations relative to prisoners of war in this Dept. On the contrary since Jan'y 1st our rations have been most materially reduced, no meat being allowed, and cornmeal substituted for flour. This reduction united to the cold and damp weather has rendered our condition peculiarly unpleasant for the last two weeks and has rendered them perhaps the most trying of all my prison experience. My health, however, holds out bravely, and I have still many comforts to be thankful for. I wrote you some time ago that the embargo upon packages designed for prisoners of war had been resumed, so you need endeavor to forward nothing to me at present. If you are able to deposit, however, a limited sum, say fifty dollars, to my credit in some banking house, either in Cleveland or New York City, notifying me with what firm you have made the deposit, I think I should be able to avail myself of it. If, however, it will embarrass you in any way do not do it.

Providence which has well provided for me thus far will, I doubt not, continue its protection as heretofore. We again hear rumors of exchange, but I have learned to be most incredulous. Should such an event take place it will take me entirely by surprise. Tell Mother and Hattie not to vex themselves about me. With the exception of a bad cold I have never been in better health. With love to all, I am,

Your Son
Henry E. Handerson

L. Handerson Esq.

Fort Pulaski, Geo. Jan'y 15th 1865

Dear Father,

Yours of the 19th ult. informing me of the shipment of a box of clothing, blankets & books for me, also of the mailing of the copy of Herodotus for which I wrote some time ago reached me on the 11th. I am sorry to say that neither of the articles has reached me, and, worse, I see but little prospect of my ever receiving them. I wrote for the clothing immediately upon the removal of the embargo upon packages, and in consequence of an opinion expressed by Col. Brown that this embargo, if renewed, would be, probably, but temporary. Immediately upon the renewal of the embargo I wrote again requesting you not to send the clothing until further advice from me. The non-receipt of the last mentioned letter in time to prevent the shipment of the clothing is most unfortunate. By my letters for the last two weeks you will have learned the condition of affairs, & that no packages are now allowed to be delivered. The only additional light on this subject since I last wrote is furnished by the following Circular from the Provost Marshal——

CIRCULAR:

Provost-Marshal's Office, Fort Pulaski, Geo.
Jan 13th 1865.

All remittances to Prisoners of War sent by permission of Brig. Gen'l Wessels, Commissary General of Prisoners, Washington D.C., and to the care of Lt. Col. John E. Mulford, Asst. Agent of Exchange, Fortress Monroe, Va., will be promptly delivered to the persons to whom they are addressed.

(Sg'd)   Frank Place, Major 157 N. Y. Vols. Provost-Marshal

If you think best to apply to Brig. Gen'l Wessels for such permission and will forward it, when obtained, to me, I will then make application to Maj. Gen'l Foster for the delivery of the box. In no other way do I see the slightest possible chance of success in an application for its delivery. Even then the matter is very doubtful. My greatest hope is that the box may be returned to you, as is sometimes done, when you can patiently await the removal of the embargo.

Your Son
H. E. Handerson

Fort Pulaski, Ga. Jan'y 22^d 1865

Dear Father,

I wrote to you last week acknowledging the receipt of yours of Dec. 19th, informing me of the shipment of a box of clothing & books for me. The box has not yet been received here, and will, in all probability, be delayed for some time, if delivered at all. On the same day that I last wrote to you I also wrote to Lieut. Col. Mulford, (through whom all packages are to be sent hereafter), asking permission to receive the box. To this communication I have as yet received no reply, and I do not expect an answer before next week. Should his reply be favorable I have little doubt that the box will be delivered speedily and safely, as Maj. Gen'l Foster has stated officially that he considers Col. Mulford's permission to receive packages equivalent to their transmission through him. Herodotus arrived safely and has contributed materially to my comfort & enjoyment. I have heard nothing from the money sent through Capt. Culp, but presume it will make its appearance in due time. Do not forward any more money to me, but if you can send me a letter of credit on some well known house in N. Y. or Baltimore I think I might be able to make use of it. The weather here has been very unpleasant during the whole month, and there is no prospect at present of any change for the better. Insufficient food & clothing have added to its discomforts, but my health continues excellent in spite of every hardship. Let me hear from you as often as possible, and I will try to write every week. With love to Mother & Hattie.

Your Son
Henry E. Handerson

L. Handerson Esq.

U. S. Military Prison, Fort Delaware, Del.
April 24th 1865

Dear Father,

Yours of the 13th inst., enclosing $25.00, is just received. Doubtless it was delayed by the recent general suspension of business consequent upon the death of President Lincoln.[42] If so desirable an event as my liberation should take place this summer, I shall not hesitate to join you at once, if such a course is permitted to me, as doubtless it would be under such circumstances. I am not at all confident, however, of any speedy release from my present confinement. Matters are now in so chaotic a state that none can tell what may be the developments of even a day. While such continues to be the case I, of course, can take no steps looking to a release other than by exchange,—which is of course equivalent to nothing. Masterly inactivity is now my only policy. Like my notorious predecesser Wilkins Micawber,[43] "The ruins of a fallen tower," I can only wait for "something to turn up." Such a position is galling enough, but I can see no honorable method of avoiding it at present. I had not intended to return to Louisiana in the event of my liberation without a consultation with you as to what plans for the future would best meet your approbation. Indeed Louisiana is now almost a wilderness, and most of my acquaintances and friends are either dead on the battle field or driven from their homes; so that I have very few inducements to return there. My health is now excellent, and I am situated, perhaps, as comfortably as I could expect. I wrote to Hattie yesterday enclosing a couple of photographs, which are said to be poor but were the best that I could procure here. I hope they may reach you safely. With best love to Mother & Hattie and wishing you all a pleasant tour through New York, I am,

Your affect. Son
Henry E. Handerson

L. Handerson Esq.
  Cleveland,
    Ohio.

U. S. Military Prison, Fort Delaware, Del.
April 27th 1865

$25.00 rec'd & receipt acknowledged some days ago.

Dear Father,

    This morning an opportunity of taking the oath of allegiance to the U.S. government, on conditions of a speedy release, has been offered, personally, to each Confederate officer here confined. I have just declined it. As this may be a decision of some importance, it is only proper that I should give you my reasons for such action. It is not worth while to bring forward now the various arguments urged for and against the right of "secession." When the war broke out I was a citizen of one of the Southern States. The citizens of that state, by their representatives in convention assembled, withdrew from the U.S. government and united themselves with their sister states of the South. Whether they had the right to "secede" is a question of little moment. They certainly had a right to throw off a form of government which they thought unjust to themselves; to "rebel" if you prefer that word. An independent government was formed, having its seat first at Montgomery, then at Richmond. To that government I swore allegiance; not only to obey its orders, but to support it against all its enemies. That that government was, and still is, unrecognized, does not obliterate the fact that it exercised all the functions of government, legislative, executive, & judicial. So long as that government is in existence I am bound by my oath to it. That it *is* still in existence is evidenced by the fact that it has two powerful armies yet in the field, and its belligerent rights, at least, are acknowledged by the U.S. in the exchange of prisoners. Therefore I owe still my allegiance to it. I do not, however, pretend to think that this must always be the case. Indeed I can no longer hope that the cause in which I am embarked is not hopeless, and, had I consulted feelings alone, I should have taken the oath when offered. I expect, when the Confederate government ceases to be, to take the oath of allegiance to the U.S., if permitted, and to become at once a law-abiding citizen. Of this intention, a perjury at the very outset would be but a poor evidence. There was, in my opinion, a spark of fine principle even in the action of "Dugald Dalgetty,"[44] who preferred to be hung rather than change his service on the day before that term of service expired. I have no reason to think, however, that this will be the last opportunity afforded us, but, if it were, I do not see how I could decide differently. Whenever the Confed. government becomes a thing of the past I shall consider my duty fully performed, and every day thereafter, spent in prison a culpable waste of time. My only embarrassment is in deciding from the lying stories of the newspapers which we are permitted to see when that event will probably occur. Let me hear from you often, and give me what reliable information you can. With love to Mother and Hattie,

H. E. Handerson.

U. S. Military Prison, Fort Delaware, Del.
May 3^d 1865

Dear Father,

In my last letter to you I stated to you my recent action with reference to the oath of allegiance, together with the reasons which constrained me to such action. As the "Southern Confederacy" is now evidently in its death struggles and even a day may bring the news of its final dissolution, you will, doubtless, be anxious to hear, as I am desirous of telling you, my determination. Of course I anticipate no release from my present confinement without previously taking the oath of allegiance to the U.S. government. Nor do I wish it. I am willing, nay anxious, to resume my allegiance as soon as it may be done consistently with honor, and, if permitted by the authorities, shall not spend an unnecessary hour in prison. As soon then as the official announcement of the surrender of the forces now under command of the Confederate general, E. Kirby Smith,[45] is received, I shall at once take such steps as will, in my opinion, secure my release most speedily. These tidings may come to-morrow and cannot, certainly, be delayed long. It cannot be a matter of more than a few weeks at farthest. From a reperusal of some of your recent letters, I conclude that it was your expectation that I might be able to meet you during your trip East. If, when released from confinement, I find myself at liberty to go where & when I please, I will endeavor to do so if you wish it. If, however, by returning immediately to Cleveland I should be able to be of any service to you in your absence, or to procure any employment for myself, I should prefer this course. It may be that we shall all be sent to the States in which we respectively enlisted. If such is to be the case I will inform you as early as possible. If you have any business acquaintance in Phila. on whom you can authorize me to draw on my arrival for an amount sufficient to enable me to carry out your wishes, please let me know at once. I shall need little in the line of clothing save some few articles of under-clothing. Let me hear from you as speedily & fully as possible. Love to all.

Your son,
Henry E. Handerson

L. Handerson, Esq.

U. S. Military Prison, Fort Delaware, Del.
May 5th 1865

Dear Father,

Yours of the 1st inst. was received yesterday. I was fully convinced of the hopelessness of the Confederate cause immediately after Lee's surrender, but did not feel at liberty to act for myself until the government, to which, in my opinion, I owed my allegiance, was beyond all doubt gone from existence. Even Johnson's surrender, which I considered a matter of course, as I do that of Dick Taylor and Kirby Smith [*]ited no new features. The simple question with me was, are Mr. Davis & his Cabinet still exercising, as far as lies in their power, the functions of government appertaining to each. I had no reliable news to the contrary, until the voluntary surrender of Mr. Mallory,[46] our Sec. of Navy. *His* action convinced me that it was time for *every one* to take care of himself, if possible. All doubts about my future course are now at an end. I shall take the oath of allegiance to the government as soon as an opportunity offers. I am now awaiting news from Washington to determine my first step in the matter. The action of the large majority of officers here has, perhaps, placed the minority in a false position of obstinacy before the authorities at the Capital, but I trust this may be overcome without serious difficulty. My views relative to my course after leaving prison I gave you tolerably fully in my last. If you wish it, and I am at liberty to do so, I will meet you all in Columbia Co. The Northern mind is at present so frenzied and beside itself with stories of projected assassinations, incendiarisms & etc. that it may not be very safe, and certainly would not be very pleasant, for me to travel very extensively. I hope your picture of the future of the South is a little overdrawn, but I recognize the justice of the leading features. I will write as often as possible.

Love to all.
Henry E. Handerson

Military Prison, Fort Delaware, Del. May 14th '65

Dear Father,

Your favors of the 4th & 10th insts. are before me. Since my last letter I have learned nothing of much importance, save that the question of the disposal of officers, prisoners of war, has not yet been definitely settled. Rumors of speedy release are abundant. Facts, on which to base them, are entirely wanting. In any event, *I* do not anticipate a personal release within less time than a month. My own application I forwarded to-day & cannot presume upon any definite reply within less time than that. The story relative to the number of officers confined here who declined taking the oath of allegiance when offered is not true. About 150 out of 2300 declined. Some of these have since applied for the oath, but my own personal acquaintance informs me of more than *two* who have yet made no application. Your plan for my future course is perfectly satisfactory, save a few details. I should prefer resuming my old occupation of teaching, (on a different scale, however, from my former method), while preparing myself for another course of medical lectures. This would relieve you of much of the expense, & would certainly be no injury to me. If the College at New Orleans is resumed on its original scale after the war, I consider it the best in the U.S., and, as I have already the tickets of one course at that institution, it might be better pecuniarily & otherwise to finish my course there. As soon as communication is opened with the interior of Louisiana I shall write at once relative to my books & other personal property there, & *may possibly* be able to hear something to my advantage in that quarter. Meanwhile I can lay down no programme of action until the action of the authorities is known. Will then endeavor to carry out your plan as far as it may be practicable. But few officers have left here yet. These few for special reasons. No general release as yet. Will write as further developments occur.

Your Son
Henry E. Handerson

Military Prison, Fort Delaware, Delaware,
May 21st 1865.

Dear Father,

I have delayed answering your interrogatories contained in Harriet's last letter for a few days, since I had expressed myself, as fully as possible at the time, with reference to them in my letter to you of the 14th inst. I addressed this letter to Clyde, and I presume you had not received it when Hattie wrote. I desired also to await further developments before coming to any decision. It is now pretty definitely ascertained that Pres't Johnson will, in the course of a few days, issue an amnesty proclamation,[47] offering pardon to all officers of the late Confederacy, below the rank of Brig. Gen'l, who shall be willing to take the oath of allegiance to the Government, under such conditions as he may prescribe. These conditions are said to be a renunciation of the doctrine of "States rights," and the abandonment of slavery. The first needs no renunciation on my part. I have never believed in it. The second I acquiesce in as a direct and unavoidable result of the war. Neither troubles my conscience. If the information above referred to is true, probably all Confed. field, staff & line officers, now in confinement, will be released within a month or six weeks. As my adhesion to the new order of things was comparatively late, I expect to be among the last to leave prison. Should you all be in Columbia Co. when I *am* released I will meet you there, if such an arrangement is satisfactory to you. If not, at any other designated point. As to the funds necessary for my traveling expenses, you can send them here with perfect safety. You can judge better than I what amount will be necessary. I shall be compelled to purchase in Phila. a complete fitout of underclothing, a hat & pair of shoes. Should think $50.00 ought to cover everything. You had better send the money as soon as possible to meet the contingency of a release sooner than I have reason to expect. I have not and cannot give you any very definite information as to my movements. As I have been for the last four years, so now I am, a creature of orders, not knowing one moment where I may be the next. What I have written is the most probable course of events, and you can safely act upon it.

Your Son
Henry E. Handerson

Military Prison, Fort Delaware, Del.
May 23^{d} 1865

Dear Father,

Yours of the 19th inst., enclosing a draft on N. Y. for $50.00, is just received. I have forwarded the draft for collection, wishing the money here ready for emergencies. The lapse of two days since I last wrote has only confirmed the opinion expressed in my last letter. The authorities on this island stated yesterday that the amnesty proclamation of Pres't Johnson was expected here daily, together with the order for the release of such prisoners of war as may see fit to avail themselves of it. The A. A. A. Gen'l of Post stated, that immediately upon the receipt of this order he would put at work a force of assistants, which would ensure the departure of all who may desire to depart within the space of a week or ten days. This is probably a little exaggerated, but it is highly probable that but few officers will remain here until the 13th June. Unless then you return to Cleveland some time before you anticipated when starting, I shall, in all probability, be able to meet you in N. Y. or elsewhere. I wrote in my last that I would meet you in Hudson. If you prefer some other point please let me know. Suppose that I am set at liberty before the 15th prox. Where shall I find you or wait for you? I may be liberated any day, but cannot approximate more nearly than I have. My reasons for preferring the Med. Col. at N. O. I will give you when I meet you. They are not unimportant, but I will, of course, do as you prefer in the matter. My old tickets will, of course, answer as evidence of one course of Med. lectures if I can procure them. They are in Louisiana, if not burned or stolen. Love to all.

Your Son
Henry E. Handerson

Military Prison, Fort Delaware, Del. May 29th '65

Dear Father,

I have just received a letter from an officer in the U.S.A. and who is now at Washington, offering if I will make an application for my release to the Sec. of War and forward it to him, to present it personally and use his best exertions to secure my release at once. I have, of course, accepted his very kind offer & have just forwarded the application. If this application is successful, (and of its success the gentleman assures me there is little or no doubt), I shall in all probability be released either the last of this week or the first of next. If I do not hear from you meanwhile I shall proceed at once to Hudson, & hope to meet you there before your return to Cleveland. Let me hear from you, if you have made other arrangements. Love to Mother & Hattie, whom I hope to meet in a few days.

Your Son,
Henry E. Handerson

L. Handerson Esq,
  Hudson,
  N. Y.

Notes to the Text

---★---

NOTES TO
Henry E. Handerson

[1] Dr. William Evans Bruner, a founder of the Academy of Medicine of Cleveland in 1902 and sole surviving early officer of the Cleveland Medical Library Association.

[2] Samuel W. Kelley, Biography of Henry Ebenezer Handerson in: Henry E. Handerson, *Gilbertus Anglicus, Medicine of the Thirteenth Century,* Cleveland, The Cleveland Medical Library Association, 1918, p. 9.

[3] H. E. Handerson, *A Contribution to the Genealogy of the Handerson Family,* New York, 1885, *passim.* There is much confusion about the spelling of the name, Handerson and Henderson being used almost interchangeably. Dr. Handerson and his descendants used the "a" consistently, but some of the collateral relatives living in the Chagrin Valley used Henderson. The crossroad at the corner of the old home at Fairmount and River Road is today called Henderson's Corners.

[4] The old home, a hospitable white frame dwelling with broad porches on either end, still stands facing the river. The present occupant, Asa Shiverick, Jr., has traced real estate records and informs me that the Handersons bought the property in 1835 for $3750. The Hon. Myron T. Herrick, former governor of Ohio and ambassador to France, purchased the farm in 1908 and built a new house further back from the river.

[5] Gertrude Van Rensselaer, ed., *Memorial to the Pioneer Women of the Western Reserve,* Cleveland, 1896, III-IV, p. 600.

[6] The late Alfred Mewett, director of the John Huntington Polytechnic Institute, owned the earliest daybook of Dr. Abijah Loveridge Dille, who started practicing medicine at Willson's Mills on September 3, 1834. Dr. Dille's daybook shows that he charged Thomas Handerson $3.00 on March 21, 1837, for "obstetrics," obviously the charge for attending the birth of Henry Ebenezer Handerson. I am indebted to the late Mr. Mewett for other Handerson data.

[7] It was located at 73 Superior Street (old numbering), which was on the north side of the street west of the Public Square and immediately east of the Wilshire Building.

[8] The Rev. Ephraim Punderson was a graduate of Union College and the General Episcopal Theological Seminary. Migrating to Ohio, he was one of the most active missionaries of the Episcopal Church, organizing a parish at Lyme in 1835, establishing Grace Church at Sandusky in the same year, and St. Paul's at Norwalk in 1836. He belonged to the High Church party. After conducting a school in Cleveland, in 1851 he was in charge of Sanger Hall, a boys' boarding school at New Hartford, N.Y., but he returned to Cleveland the following year. *The Fire Lands Pioneer,* N.S., 1882 I, 161-62.

[9] H. E. Handerson, History of Grace Church, in: *Past and Present of Grace Church,* Cleveland, Ohio, 1898, p. 19.

[10] The business of Handerson and Punderson descended through a number of successors and eventually became Strong Cobb & Company, Inc., drug manufacturers and wholesalers.

[11] At the Junior Exhibition in 1857 he delivered the Greek Oration entitled "Death of Socrates." The manuscript, finely penned, is preserved in the Cleveland Medical Library. While at Hobart, he was a charter member of the local chapter of Theta Delta Chi.

[12] In his class of 95 graduates, 28 (almost 30 percent) held degrees from liberal arts colleges. Service in the Federal cause was noted in the official list of alumni, but Handerson's Confederate record does not appear. *Catalogue of the Alumni, Officers & Fellows. 1807-1891.* College of Physicians & Surgeons in the City of New York. New York, 1891.

[13] Mrs. Henry E. Handerson died in Cleveland July 6, 1955, at the age of 94. Philip C. Handerson, the sole surviving son, lives in Delray, Florida.

[14] Note introducing H. E. Handerson, Gilbert of England and His "Compendium Medicine," *Medical Pickwick,* 1915, I, 118.

[15] *Ibid.*

[16] Medical Cleveland by H. E. Handerson, M.D., in: S. P. Orth, *A History of Cleveland,* Chicago and Cleveland, 1910, I, pp. 176-216. Medical Cleveland in the Nineteenth Century, *Cleveland Medical Journal,* 1909, VIII, 59-72; 146-56; 208-18.

[17] The Medical Department of Ohio Wesleyan was consolidated with the Medical Department of Western Reserve University in 1910. See Frederick C. Waite, *Western Reserve University Centennial History of the School of Medicine,* Cleveland, 1946, p. 387 ff.

[18] See footnote 2.

[19] Shifting of population gradually deprived Grace Church of its support, and it was merged into its mother church, now Trinity Cathedral.

[20] George Franklin Smythe, *A History of the Diocese of Ohio until the Year 1918,* Cleveland, 1931, p. 481; *Journals of Conventions, Diocese of Ohio,* Cleveland, 1886 to 1918, inclusive.

[21] See footnote 9.

[22] Minutes of the organizations mentioned are in the custody of the Cleveland Medical Library Association. See also Clyde L. Cummer, Medical Societies in Cleveland from 1890 to 1945, *Ohio State Archeological and Historical Society Quarterly,* 1948, October, 356-64.

[23] Handerson served the Cleveland Medical Library Association in the following capacities, viz.: trustee, 1894-1914; president, 1896-1902; treasurer, April 8, 1895; asst. treasurer, March 8, 1895; executive committee, 1903-1911; house committee, 1903-1905; finance, 1905-1906, 1908-1913; building committee, 1906; historical committee, 1908.

[24] Harvey Cushing, "The Doctor and His Books," an address delivered at the dedication of the Dudley P. Allen Memorial Medical Library, Cleveland, November 13, 1926, pp. 27-28. Reprinted in Harvey Cushing, *Consecratio Medici and Other Papers,* Boston, 1928, p. 259.

[25] Under the leadership of Genevieve Miller, PH.D. and Henry H. Fertig, M.D., the Handerson Medical History Society was organized as an unofficial project of the Cleveland Medical Library Association on December 14, 1953.

[26] *The Medical Pickwick,* 1915, I, 118-20.

[27] Henry E. Handerson, *Gilbertus Anglicus, Medicine of the Thirteenth Century*. With a Biography of the Author. Published posthumously for private distribution. Cleveland, Ohio, The Cleveland Medical Library Association, 1918, 77 pp.

[28] *Proceedings of the Tenth Annual Meeting of the Immortal 600*. Richmond, Virginia, June 1, 2, and 3, 1915. Richmond, 1915.

[29] According to Dr. W. E. Bruner, his blindness resulted from glaucoma.

[30] On May 30, 1956, under the leadership of Mrs. Walter C. White, the Cleveland chapters of the United Daughters of the Confederacy dedicated with appropriate services a Confederate marker on Dr. Handerson's grave in Lot 8, Section 3, of Woodland Cemetery in Cleveland.

Yankee in Gray

[1] Virgil, *Aeneid*, Book I, 203: "The day may dawn when this plight shall be sweet to remember."

[2] Approximate date 1890-1895.

[3] Sanger Hall [Author's note].

[4] Approximately forty miles northwest of Chattanooga on the Cumberland Plateau.

[5] The Louisiana State Military Academy opened on January 1, 1860. In 1869 it moved to Baton Rouge and became the Louisiana State University in 1870.

[6] Dr. Thomas Hunt had founded the Medical College of Louisiana in 1834. It became the Medical Department of the University of Louisiana in 1845, and just before the Civil War New Orleans was the third largest medical center in the United States. See William Frederick Norwood, *Medical Education in the United States before the Civil War*, Philadelphia, 1944, pp. 363-68.

[7] Warren Stone (1808-1872), a native of St. Albans, Vt., had received his M.D. degree in 1831 at the Berkshire Medical Institution, Pittsfield, Mass. Befriended by Dr. Thomas Hunt when he first came to New Orleans, he eventually became Professor of Surgery at the University of Louisiana. See Howard A. Kelly and Walter L. Burrage, *Dictionary of American Medical Biography*, New York-London, 1928, p. 1174.

[8] Tobias Gibson Richardson (1827-1892), Professor of Anatomy at the University of Louisiana, had been a student of Samuel D. Gross at Louisville, Ky. *Ibid.*, p. 1034.

[9] Augustus H. Cenas taught obstetrics and diseases of women and children. See Norwood, *op. cit.*, p. 364.

[10] Thomas Hunt (1808-1867) was born in Charleston, S. C. and received his medical degree from the University of Pennsylvania in 1829. See Kelly and Burrage, *op. cit.*, pp. 619-20.

[11] John Pintard Davidson (1812-1890) had graduated from the University of Pennsylvania Medical School in 1832. *Ibid.*, pp. 298-99.

[12] Adelina Patti (1843-1919) was one of the greatest sopranos of the nineteenth century.

[13] John Bell (1797-1869) of Tennessee was Presidential candidate of the Constitutional Union Party in 1860 with Edward Everett (1794-1865), the famous orator, as Vice-Presidential candidate. See *Dictionary of American Biography*, II, pp. 157-58; VI, pp. 223-26.

[14] John Cabell Breckenridge (1821-1875) from Kentucky, Vice-President of the United States from 1857 to 1861, who subsequently became Secretary of War of the Confederacy. See *Dictionary of American Biography*, III, pp. 7-10.

[15] On the retreat from Drury's Bluff in a stampede of his own command, see "Military Memoirs of a Confederate" p. 595. Note 1. By Gen. E. P. Alexander [Author's note].

[16] Dr. Clark was living in Baltimore in 1901 [Author's note].

[17]See H. E. Handerson letter, April 4, 1861, p. 87.

[18]These letters are reproduced beginning on p. 87.

[19]Letter of July 1, 1861, p. 88.

[20]Stafford Guards. 1861.

    Capt.—L. A. Stafford

    1st Lieut.—Smith Gordon

    2d   ”   —C. D. Waters

    Jr. 2d Lieut.—W. T. Cummings, Jr.

    1st Sergt.—G. D. Workman

    2d   ”   —A. C. Bringhurst

    3d   ”   —N. C. Weems, Jr.

    4th   ”   —Archie Gordon

    1st Corp.—Wm. Swilley

    2d   ”   —C. R. Hayworth

    3d   ”   —Geo. Blair

    4th   ”   Robt. Cruikshank

    Ensign—Henry Erwin   [Author's note]

[21]Dr. Smith Gordon of Alexandria—Still living (1901) [Author's note].

[22]He was killed in the affair of Mine Run, Nov. 27th, 1863 [Author's note].

[23]Ninth Regiment La. Vols.

    Col.—Richard Taylor

    Lt. Col.—E. G. Randolph

    Major—N. G. Walker

    Mustered into state service July 6, 1861 [Author's note].

[24]Richard Taylor (1826-1879) had a sugar plantation in Saint Charles Parish, La. called "Fashion." Widely read in English and French literature, he collected and studied the works of great military men. *Dictionary of American Biography*, XVIII, pp. 340-41.

[25]Letter of July 18, 1861, see p. 89.

[26]On July 25th, 1861, the 8th Brigade, 1st Corps, Army of the Potomac, was organized by Gen. Beauregard, as follows:

        Col. J. G. Seymour, Commanding.

      6th La. Regt.—Col. J. G. Seymour,

      7th La. “   —Col. Harry Hays,

      8th “   “   —Col. H. B. Kelly,

      9th “   “   —Col. Richard Taylor,

      1st La. Special Battln.—Maj. C. R. Wheat.

On Oct. 22d, 1861, the Louisiana Brigade was under the command of Brig. Gen. Richard Taylor and was known as the 5th Brigade, 3d Division, (Maj. Genl. Longstreet), Potomac District, Dept. N. Va. [Author's note].

[27]Brig. Gen. W. H. T. Walker (1816-1864), a career soldier, graduate of the U.S. Military Academy in 1837, was one of the most experienced officers to enter the Confederate army. See *Dictionary of American Biography*, XIX, p. 365.

[28]Roberdeau Chatham Wheat. For an account of his military career see Richard Taylor, *Destruction and Reconstruction, Personal Experiences of the Late War*. Ed. By Richard B. Harwell, New York, 1955, passim.

[29]Narciso Lopez (1798-1851) in 1850 attempted to secure Cuban independence from Spain by landing at Cárdenas with an armed band organized in the United States.

[30]William Walker (1824-1860), a military adventurer who had become powerful in

Nicaragua in the 1850's. After having been overthrown and having fled to the United States, he made several efforts to return, on the last of which he landed in Honduras, was captured and executed.

31 Capt. Dugald Dalgetty was a soldier of fortune in Sir Walter Scott's *Legend of Montrose*.

32 Taylor, *op. cit.*, pp. 22-23.

33 "Alsatia" was a district in Whitefriars, London, in the 17th century situated between Fleet Street and the Thames, where criminals had the privilege of sanctuary. It figured in Sir Walter Scott's *The Fortunes of Nigel* and was ruled by Duke Hildebrod, an innkeeper. "Duke Hildebrod . . . was a monstrously fat old man, with only one eye; and a nose which bore evidence to the frequency, strength, and depth of his potations."

34 Taylor, *op. cit.*, p. 21.

35 A term used originally for buccaneers on the Spanish American coasts which was later given to adventurers who took part in military expeditions against countries with which their own countries were at peace.

36 See letter of September 11, 1861, p. 90.

37 This may have been Dr. John T. Jones, listed by Wyndham B. Blanton, *Medicine in Virginia in the Nineteenth Century* (Richmond, 1933), p. 406, as commissioned assistant surgeon, February 5, 1862 "in hospitals at Warrenton, Ashland and Gordonsville, Va., promoted to surgeon August 20, 1864."

38 See letter p. 92.

39 See letter of January 19, 1862, p. 92.

40 See letter of March 5, 1862, p. 93.

41 Juvenal, *Satires*, X, 22: "The traveller with empty pockets will sing even in the robber's face."

42 For a parallel account see Handerson letter, July 13, 1862, p. 95.

43 April 24, 1862—Capt. Stafford was commissioned Colonel of the 9th La. Regt. [Author's note].

44 Brig. Gen. Geo. H. Steuart commanded the First Maryland Regiment. Arnold Elzey (1816-1871) was a West Point graduate in 1837 and a veteran of the Mexican War. On April 25, 1861 he resigned his captaincy in the U.S. Army and joined the Confederates with the rank of Colonel. After distinguishing himself in the first battle of Bull Run, he was promoted to Brigadier General. *National Cyclopedia of American Biography*, 1929, VI, p. 217.

Isaac Ridgeway Trimble (1802-1888), graduate of West Point in 1822. He joined the Confederate army as Colonel of engineers and constructed the Norfolk defences. He took part in Pickett's charge at Gettysburg where he lost a leg. *Dictionary of American Biography*, 1936, XVIII, pp. 641-42.

Richard Stoddert Ewell (1817-1872), West Point graduate in 1840, had seen service in the Mexican War. He resigned on May 7, 1861 and became a Colonel in the Confederate army. An able and energetic officer, he served in many campaigns including the Valley, Cedar Mountain, Manassas Junction, Gettysburg, the first Wilderness engagement, and subsequently Richmond, which he commanded when it was evacuated. *Dictionary of American Biography*, 1931, VI, pp. 229-30.

45 A conical rifle bullet which had been invented by Capt. C. E. Minié of France.

46 Col. John R. Kenly, commander of the First Maryland Infantry. It was erroneously reported in the official dispatch that he was killed in this engagement. See *War of the Rebellion*, Series I, Vol. XII, Pt. I, p. 525. He was severely wounded and taken prisoner.

The full description of the battle at Front Royal is in *Ibid.*, pp. 536-37, 555-58. For the Confederate report by Brig. Gen. Richard Taylor, see *Ibid.*, pp. 800-1.

47 Major General Nathaniel Prentiss Banks (1816-1894), former Speaker of the House of Representatives and Governor of Massachusetts, was commanding the Department of the Shenandoah, U.S. Army.

48 The Official Reports of the battles at Front Royal, Middletown, Winchester, Cross Keys & port Republic will be found in *"War of the Rebellion,"* Series I, Vol. XII, Part I, pp. 524 et seq. These references will be marked W. R. throughout this paper. See W. R. op. cit. pp. 572-3 [Author's note].

Charles H. T. Collis was Captain, Commanding Zouaves d'Afrique, Body Guard.

49 "On the morning of the 25th, being ordered by Major-General Jackson to execute a flank movement upon the enemy's strong position in front of Winchester, the brigade was formed into line of battle in the face of a severe fire of artillery and musketry, the Seventh Regiment acting as a reserve. The advance and subsequent charge were both conducted steadily and in good order, resulting in the dislodgment of the enemy and the capture of the town." Report of Brig. Gen. Richard Taylor, May 26, 1862, in W. R., *loc. cit.*, pp. 800-1.

50 John Charles Frémont (1813-1890), the famous explorer of the West, who came in command of the army in Western Virginia. Brig. Gen. James Shields (1806-1879), commanded the First Division of the Department of the Rappahannock.

When Bank's force was driven from Front Royal by Jackson, President Lincoln ordered Frémont to march from the Mountain Department and reinforce him. See W. R., *loc. cit.*, p. 643.

51 Cross Keys June 8, Port Republic June 9 [Author's note].

See Frémont's report of these bloody engagements, *Ibid.*, pp. 653-55. A peppery report of errors and poor planning was given by Brig. Gen. Shields, *Ibid.*, pp. 684-85.

52 The reports of the "Seven Day Battles" will be found in W. R., Series I, Vol. XI, Part II. Gen. Lee's Report p. 489; Gen. Ewell's Report p. 605; Gen. Stafford's Report p. 619 [Author's note].

53 Col. I. G. Seymour commanded the Sixth Louisiana regiment. "On the afternoon of Friday, the 27th ultimo, in the charge at Cold Harbor, Colonel Seymour was shot from his horse and died a few minutes after." Report of Col. Leroy A. Stafford, W.R., Ser. I, Vol. XI, Part II, p. 620.

54 Major C. R. Wheat, killed June 27.

55 John Bell Hood (1831-1879), a graduate of West Point, had served under Robert E. Lee in Texas. After joining the Confederate army, he was made Brigadier General in command of the "Texas Brigade." *Dictionary of American Biography*, 1932, IX, pp. 193-94.

56 James Fenimore Cooper (1789-1851), author of the Leather Stocking Tales: *The Deerslayer, The Last of the Mohicans, The Pathfinder, The Pioneers, The Prairie.*

57 See Handerson's letters to his father and sister, July 12 and 13, 1862, pp. 94-97.

58 Gordonsville July 19, 1862 [Author's note].

59 Major-General John Pope, U.S.A., commanded the Army of Virginia. On September 5, 1862 his army was consolidated with the Army of the Potomac under Major-General George B. McClellan, and Pope was relieved of his command.

60 Described in his note to his father of September 10, 1862, see p. 99.

61 ". . . we encountered the shells from three of the enemy's batteries, and had the misfortune about dark to lose several of our number, among whom was the gallant young

Gordon, a lieutenant in the Ninth Louisiana Regiment and acting assistant adjutant-general of the brigade, who was killed by a shell which cut off both his legs at the thigh." Report of E. Pendleton, W.R., Ser. I, Vol. XIX, Pt. II, p. 1016.

[62] See Handerson letter, November 6, 1862, p. 99.

[63] See Report of Brigadier-General Hays in W.R., Ser. I, Vol. XXI, pp. 674-75.

[64] Major-General Ambrose E. Burnside, Commander of the Army of the Potomac.

[65] See Handerson letters of January 14 and 18, 1863, pp. 100-01.

[66] Major-General Joseph Hooker had superseded Major-General Burnside in command of the Army of the Potomac on January 26, 1863.

[67] Major-General Jubal A. Early. See his report in W.R., Ser. I, Vol. XXV, Pt. I, pp. 1000-2.

[68] Brigadier-General William Barksdale. See *Ibid.*, pp. 839-41.

[69] Brigadier-General John Gibbon. See his report, *Ibid.*, pp. 350-51.

[70] This was Hazel Run and our charge was made towards the north, almost perpendicularly to the Orange plank road [Author's note]. See Handerson letter of May 13, 1863, p. 101.

[71] This is described briefly in Early's report. See W.R., Ser. I, Vol. XXV, Pt. I, pp. 1001-2.

[72] This was the Orange & Fredericksburg turnpike [Author's note].

[73] See Handerson letter of May 13, 1863, p. 101.

[74] Major-General George E. Pickett.

[75] See Brigadier-General Hays' report in W.R., Ser. I, Vol. XXVII, Pt. II, pp. 479-82.

[76] Lt. R. T. Crawford.

[77] 1st La.—Maj. Jas. Neligan comd'g.
     2d " —Col. J. M. Williams "
     10th " —Col. J. M. Legget, Maj. H. D. Monier
     14th " —Lt. Col. D. Zable comd'g.
     15th " —Col. Ed. Pendleton "   [Author's note]

[78] Boarman is now (1901) one of the judges of the U.S. District Court of Louisiana. His political career has been checkered; he was at one time a bitter Republican and opponent of his old companions in arms [Author's note].

[79] Merrick is now (1901) on the staff of Gov. Heard of La. in Baton Rouge [Author's note].

[80] "I regret to say that Capt. D. T. Merrick, of the staff, was seriously wounded in the head while gallantly cheering on the line to the charge." Report of Brig.-Gen. L. A. Stafford [written by H. E. Handerson], December 5, 1863. W.R., Ser. I, Vol. XXIX, Pt. I, p. 872.

[81] An official report of the part taken by our brigade in this so-called battle of "Payne's Farm," signed, of course, by Gen. Stafford, but bearing the ear-marks of my pen, will be found in the collection entitled *"War of the Rebellion. Official Records of Union and Confederate Armies."* Series I, Vol. XXIX, Part I, Reports, pp. 870-71. On the following pages to 876 will be found the reports of the various regimental commanders of our brigade, addressed to me as Assistant Adjutant General, though my name is incorrectly spelled Henderson [Author's note].

[82] Alexandria, La., was captured by Gen. Banks March 15, 1864. The battles of Mansfield and Pleasant Hill took place April 8 and 9, 1864, and Alexandria was evacuated May 14, 1864, just nine days after my capture in "The Wilderness [Author's note].

[83] William Swinton, *Campaigns of the Army of the Potomac*, New York, 1866, p. 401.

[84] Ewell's report of this battle may be read in W. R., Ser. I, Vol. XXXVI, Pt. I, pp. 1069-75.

[85] Major-General John Sedgwick commanded the Sixth Army Corps, U.S. Army.

[86] Brigadier-General Albin Schoepf. On June 2, 1864 the prison contained 8,124 prisoners, with accommodations for 2,500 more. See Report of W. Hoffman, W.R., Ser. II, Vol. VII, p. 187. A graphic description of prison life at Fort Delaware was written by the Rev. Isaac W.K. Handy, *United States Bonds; Or Duress by Federal Authority. A Journal of Current Events during an Imprisonment of Fifteen Months at Fort Delaware*, Baltimore, 1874.

[87] See Handerson letter of June 13, 1864, p. 103.

Handy, *loc. cit.*, p. 482 reported this class: "A class in Greek and Latin is now in full operation, taught by Capt. Henderson, of Louisiana. Among the students, of whom there are twelve, are Captain Gordon, Dye, Dunkle, G. L. Roberts, and Mackey."

[88] See letters of August 13, 14, and 18, 1864, pp. 104-05.

[89] The captain and the second mate were court-martialed and found guilty of "neglect of duty" for this incident, which was thought to have been part of a rebel plot to enable them to escape. W.R., Ser. I, Vol. XXXV, Pt. I, p. 23.

[90] Major-General J. G. Foster, U.S. Army, reported on August 26, 1864 that "The camp for the 600 rebel prisoners of war has been selected, and I am now having a strong fence put up around it to prevent any possibility of escape; this camp will be ready in a few days, and I propose to take the prisoners up at once. The 600 prisoners of war (rebel) arrived yesterday in the U.S. Steam transport Crescent, and are now in the harbor." *Ibid.*, pp. 22-23.

[91] See Handerson letter of September 8, 1864, p. 106.

For an account of the prisoners, see J. Ogden Murray, *The Immortal Six Hundred. A Story of Cruelty to Confederate Prisoners of War*, Winchester, Va., 1905.

[92] "The rebels, in firing on Morris Island, do not endeavor to avoid this camp, and although the shot and shell fall all around no one has as yet received any injury. The prisoners seem to be perfectly contented with their lot. They receive the same treatment and rations as our prisoners now in Charleston." Report of Major-General J. G. Foster, September 19, 1864, W.R., Ser. I, Vol. XXXV, Pt. I, p. 24.

[93] See Handerson letters of October 30 and November 27, 1864, pp. 106-107. The order to move the prisoners was given on October 20, 1864 and the 157th N. Y. Volunteers were assigned duty as guards. Cf. W.R., Ser. I, Vol. XXXV, Pt. 2, pp. 314-15.

"The removal was made Oct. 21, 1864. We landed at Fort Pulaski, Oct. 23ᵈ, 1864" [Author's note].

[94] Philip P. Brown, Jr. was ordered to command Fort Pulaski on November 1, 1864. Special orders No. 378, *Ibid.*, p. 322.

[95] Quincy Adams Gillmore (1825-1888), Major-General commanding the Dept. of the South from Hilton Head, S. C., graduated from West Point in 1849. He conducted successful seige operations against Charleston. Cf. *National Cyclopaedia of American Biography*, 1897, Vol. IV, pp. 54-55; *Dictionary of American Biography*, 1931, Vol. VII, p. 295.

[96] See Handerson letters of December 4 and 14, 1864, p. 108.

[97] Col. P. P. Brown, Jr. 157 N. Y. Vols.

Lt. Col. James E. Carmichael [Author's note].

[98] Edward Leslie Molineux (1833-1915) had a distinguished war record. Cf. *National Cyclopaedia of American Biography*, 1921, Vol. II, p. 252: "He was promoted brigadier-general by brevet for conspicuous gallantry and zeal at Fisher's Hill, Winchester and Cedar Creek."

99 On February 1, 1865 Gen. C. Grover, commanding the District of Savannah, reported that his medical director had inspected the conditions at Fort Pulaski and reported "that they are in a condition of great suffering and exhaustion for the want of sufficient food and clothing; also that they have the scurvy to a considerable extent." He recommended that they be put on full rations and be allowed to receive clothing from their friends. W.R., Ser. II, Vol. VIII, p. 163. "Full rations restored Feb'y 12, 1865" [Author's note].

100 On February 14, 1865, W. Hoffman, Commissary-General of Prisoners in Washington, wrote to General Grant suggesting that the 600 rebel officers at Fort Pulaski be exchanged for an equal number of Northern officers held near Charleston. Grant replied that he had already authorized Maj. Gen. J. G. Foster, commanding the Dept. of the South, to exchange all prisoners under his command. "I have not yet heard from him on the subject, but presume he will carry out my instructions as promptly as possible." W.R., Ser. II, Vol. VIII, pp. 218-19. In a subsequent letter of March 21 Grant stated: "I do not know what has been done with the officers at Fort Pulaski. I sent orders to have them delivered at Charleston. Before the order was received Charleston had fallen into our possession. I then sent orders to have them sent to the James River. Before that order was received General Gillmore wrote to me that, having received my first order, which had been directed to General Foster, he had sent a flag to find an enemy to deliver the prisoners to. I have heard nothing since." *Ibid.,* p. 419.

101 We left Fort Pulaski March 4, 1865.
Reached Fort Delaware March 12, 1865 [Author's note].

102 Capt. Park in his Diary says "March 13th to 15th"—see "Southern Historical Society Papers," III, p. 124 [Author's note].

103 Of 7,126 prisoners at Ft. Delaware on May 31, 1865, during the month of June 41 died and 6,977 were released. W.R., Ser. II, Vol. VIII, p. 1002.

104 Lucan, *Works,* I, 128: "The conquering cause was pleasing to the gods, but the conquered one to Cato."

Wartime Letters

[1] His sister, Harriet Handerson.

[2] J. Routh Williams.

[3] Rev. Caleb Dowe, the Episcopalian rector of Alexandria parish.

[4] Mr. Washington Compton, a cotton planter of Alexandria, La.

[5] Gen. G. Mason Graham.

[6] The convention had assembled at Montgomery, Ala. on February 4, 1861 to form the Confederate government.

[7] Ebenezer Punderson, Jr., his aunt's brother, who was a business partner of Lewis Handerson in the drug store of Handerson and Punderson.

[8] Leroy A. Stafford.

[9] John Compton, eldest son of Washington Compton, who had been a fellow medical student with him in New Orleans in the fall of 1860. However, he failed to appear at Camp Moore.

[10] His foster parents were then living at Beersheba Springs, Grundy Co.

[11] See *frontispiece*.

[12] Col. Richard Taylor. See note 24, p. 125.

[13] E. G. Randolph and N. G. Walker.

[14] Pierre Gustave Toutant Beauregard (1818-1893), a graduate of West Point in 1838, had just been appointed Superintendent of the Academy and resigned to become Brigadier-General in the Confederate Army. He had directed the bombardment of Fort Sumter, S. C.

[15] Algerian infantry troops of the French army who wore a colorful uniform. Several Civil War companies in both armies imitated them.

[16] Leonidas Polk (1806-1864), Bishop of Louisiana of the Protestant Episcopal Church, resigned his bishopric in 1861 to become a major general in the Confederate army. He was killed in a battle near Pine Mountain, Ga. on June 14, 1864. Cf. *D.A.B.*, 1935, XV, 39-40.

[17] See note 7.

[18] On August 6, 1861 Congress had passed a mild law providing for the seizure of property which was used to aid the rebellion. The much more drastic "second confiscation act" of the following year was rarely enforced.

[19] Brig. Gen. W. H. T. Walker, see note 27, p. 125.

[20] Col. Richard Taylor, see note 24, p. 125.

[21] James Newman.

[22] Combining armies and gunboats the Union forces carried on a "river war" on the Tennessee and Cumberland, gaining control of Nashville and forcing the Confederate army to withdraw from Kentucky.

[23] Brigadier-General Don Carlos Buell (1818-1898), commander of the Army of the Ohio,

was in charge of operations in central and eastern Tennessee. The following month, on April 7, he joined Grant to repulse the Confederate forces at Shiloh, Tenn. He was replaced by Rosecrans on October 30, 1862 because he failed to stop the Confederate advance into Kentucky which was led by General Braxton Bragg.

[24] Fort Henry, on the Tennessee River, had been captured by Grant on February 6, 1862, while Fort Donelson on the Cumberland River fell on February 16.

[25] Senator Lyman Trumbull of Illinois. See note 18.

[26] Fort Warren in Boston harbor was where James M. Mason and John Slidell, the Confederate ambassadors to Great Britain and France, had been held by Union forces.

[27] Major-General James E. B. Stuart. See the report of his Maryland campaign in W.R., Ser. I, Vol. 19, Pt. I, pp. 814-21.

[28] On August 28, 1862 Gen. Braxton Bragg had begun to march north from Chattanooga to invade Kentucky. Gen. J. H. Morgan carried out costly raids near Nashville in August.

[29] Gen. Benjamin F. Butler, referred to as "Beast Butler" by southerners. New Orleans had been captured in April 1862 by a fleet led by Farragut, and Butler occupied the city with an army of 18,000. He subjected the city to irresponsible martial law and the confiscation of property. Among his excesses was the execution of a citizen for tearing down the Union flag. He was replaced by Gen. N. P. Banks on December 17, 1862.

[30] The official count was 12,085 enlisted men and 435 officers. See W.R., Ser. I, Vol. 19, Pt. I, p. 549.

[31] The bloody battle of Perryville on October 8, 1862, although not a decisive Northern victory, led Bragg to withdraw his army into Tennessee.

[32] Brigadier-General Harry T. Hays, commanding First Louisiana Brigade.

[33] John C. Hays, a famous Indian fighter in Texas, who had also distinguished himself in the Mexican War. *National Cyclopaedia of American Biography*, 1921, II, 241.

[34] McMinnville, Tenn.

[35] He had evidently taken the furlough mentioned in the letter of January 18.

[36] Rose O'Neal Greenhow (d. 1864) was a famous Confederate spy who was a popular Washington socialite during the early days of the war and used her position to obtain military information for the South. After imprisonment in Capitol Hill prison she was exiled to Richmond where she helped Miss Emily Mason, sister of James M. Mason in hospital work. See Ishbel Ross, *Rebel Rose, Life of Rose O'Neal Greenhow, Confederate Spy* (New York, 1954), pp. 236-237. She also published an account of her experiences in *My Imprisonment and the First Year of Abolition Rule at Washington*, London, 1863.

[37] E. W. Palmer of Cleveland.

[38] His foster uncle, the Rev. Ephraim Punderson, whose boarding school at New Hartford, N. Y., he had attended.

[39] Hilton Head, S. C., the headquarters of the Department of the South.

[40] Rev. Richard Berry, Episcopalian clergyman.

[41] Gideon B. Perry, rector of St. Paul's Episcopal Parish.

[42] Lincoln had died on April 15.

[43] A character in Dickens' *David Copperfield*.

[44] See note 31, p. 126.

[45] Gen. E. Kirby Smith, in command of Confederate forces beyond the Mississippi, surrendered at New Orleans on May 26, 1865.

[46] S. R. Mallory of Florida. He was imprisoned for a short time and then released.

[47] The proclamation was made on May 29, 1865.

This book was composed in Baskerville types
and printed on Perkins & Squier RRR paper
by Davis & Warde, Inc., Pittsburgh.
Bound in G.S.B. cloth
by Russell-Rutter Company, Inc., New York City.
Design and typography by Merald E. Wrolstad.